WHAT HAPPENED TO THE MAN NEXT DOOR?

A Tragic Story of False Allegations, Police Negligence, and How Idiocy In Massachusetts Social Services Destroyed A Family

Mark A. Wilmot

Disclaimer
The contents of this book are based on official agency documents, court records, evidence presented for trials, and the author's opinions and analysis, which are well-founded statements based on facts, the publishing of which constitutes protected free speech under established law. Legal thresholds of preventing libel, consistent with case law and established publishing standards have been met

Credits
Images not owned by the author are public property, courtesy of the National Archives. Quotes, passages, and poems are attributed to their sources, or are sections of public court documents, or are available through the Freedom of Information Act.

Availability of the Author
The author plans a nationwide speaking, training, and education tour during 2010-2013 to share this tragic story with legal professionals and public servants employed by law enforcement and social service agencies. Contact the author directly for rates & reservations, and information.

Table of Contents

INTRODUCTION

The Fog of War

I'm an American man writing this book. What you are about to read are my private thoughts and analysis during a time of deep sadness and shock in my life. These thoughts occurred when I was suddenly and illegally forced into exile away from my home and family. As I begin writing, it's been more than fifty days since it happened. The exile began when an attack was made on my family, the Wilmot family of Oxford, Massachusetts. Don't make the mistake of believing that I'm simply using the analogy of an attack to gain your attention and sympathy. An attack really did occur. It was carried out by unfriendly people who used any means necessary to accomplish their objectives. The use of terror was involved too: Would you be terrified if government workers showed up at your door without warning, gained entry to your home, inspected your belongings, accused you of a serious crime, placed a gag order on your family, threatened to take your children away if you returned home, filed documents with faulty information at the local district court to justify having a warrant

1

issued, and then conspired to have you arrested on a Friday evening and thrown into jail over the Fourth of July weekend, and finally, if those same people broke up your family in a manner which caused your family to endure great pain and suffering?

That is exactly what happened to me and my family, and that is what this narrative is about.

In the aftermath of the unwarranted attack against a man and his family exists the analogous fog of war, a condition where chaos exists, when normal routines are upset by commotion, and reliable information is hard to find. Objects, movements, and people's actions become difficult to discern, making it hard to tell who is friend or foe, and what is good, and what is evil.

What is known in this situation is that a *repugnant* violation of a family's privacy, unity, and lawful right to associate with each other was carried out against a good family, which was headed by a man who served his country honorably and faithfully as a United States Marine for many years.

Now that an attack occurred, there must be assessments, casualty reports, hasty surveys, and adjustments to all things that matter. Marines train for scenarios of reduced awareness which occur during times of chaos. To overcome it, we learn that we must rely on our intellect, training, experience, sense of honor, and *will to survive and succeed*. So, despite the chaos caused by this most unexpected encroachment into the arena of liberty and family sanctity, despite my deep emotional wounds and loss of sleep, and despite the weeks of siege and isolation that have followed, I've had time to gain clarity and understanding. People and their actions in this case fall to one side or the other. There is no gray area, no in-between zone. As read this account and analysis of this tragedy, I challenge you to choose a side to be on and then take action.

IF THIS WAS AN ATTACK, THEN WHO IS THE ENEMY?

If the family in this story was indeed attacked, the immediate question is by whom? In this instance, the attack was conducted by people employed by state government agencies. Call them public servants, government agents, or social workers, it does not really matter how they are labeled. At this early stage of the event, the public servants involved may not even comprehend they have done wrong. Many of those involved are obviously overzealous, yet complacent or ignorant about their responsibilities. Perhaps they have become accustomed too *not being held accountable* to the people they are supposed to serve. Somehow, someway, they must come to understand that requirement. They must come to realize that it is immoral and disrespectful to attack a man and his family in their home on a holiday, especially when there are two Marines within that family, who have sacrificed portions of their life to uphold the Constitution and its principles of freedom. The point here is that United States Marines swear to an oath to defeat all enemies, both foreign and domestic. In this case, idiocy and wrongful actions of misdirected public servants are the enemy. If you understand this position, then you will agree that just like the enemy of terrorism, the enemy of idiocy must be taken on, and defeated. The reasons why government actions were wrong and illegal are explained throughout this story. Accepted case law is cited. It's important to note that no matter what anyone says or thinks, Constitutional law remains the legal foundation of the United States of America, and its authority supercedes all else.

A New Mission In Life Emerges

This attack has stricken me to the very core of whom I am and what I have come to stand for as a person. Now is not a good time for me to surrender to principles, especially when one knows they are correct. I consider the implications of what is happening to my family, and to others, and begin to realize that a new mission in my life is emerging. It's not a mission I would have chosen for myself – but instead a serious task which must be accomplished.

This new mission includes four distinct components:

First, I must take care of my wounded family as best I can, and take care of myself too.

Secondly, I must go about the task of informing the public of things gone awry, while defending myself from the falsehoods manufactured against me.

Third, the new mission does not stop with the objectives above because it's not just about me and my family; the gross injustice which you are about to learn about could happen to anyone else, yes, even you, if the idiocy behind it is not defeated. That being the truth, I must work toward causing positive, and rightful change in government services by educating public servants of the impact of misguided and wrongful actions.

Last, but not least, the new mission in my life includes restoring my reputation, and ultimately, achieving a meaningful victory by attaining retribution to compensate for the extraordinary damage done to members of my family.

ATTENTION ALL PARENTS: THIS COULD HAPPEN TO YOU!

Parents Mark and Theresa Wilmot

Consider This:

Prior to the events of Mother's Day 2009, the six-member Wilmot Family of Oxford, Massachusetts enjoyed each other's company and support. They ate breakfasts, suppers, and dinners together. They attended church on Sunday, nurtured and supported each other without reservation, and without complaint of abuse. It was a connected, supportive, vibrant family. The home was clean, and the family was intact, and functioning as a typical working class family does. In the eyes of many, the family was a *jewel* of a family – a family that many others wished they could have. As the head of this family, I would have done anything to protect it, but as events unfolded, I found myself to be one man of insufficient means facing the power and resources of local and state agencies, staffed by people with a predisposition against men's rights and family rights, and a sagacious predisposition retarded by idiocy and ignorance of Constitutional Law.

Established Case Law

United States vs. Lee, 106 U.S. 196, 220 (1882).

"No man in this country is so high that he is above the law. No officer of the law may set that law at defiance with impunity. All the officers of the government, from the highest to the lowest, (including social workers and police officers) are creatures of the law and are bound to obey it. It is the only supreme power in our system of government, and every man or woman, who by accepting office, participates in its functions is only the more strongly bound to submit to that supremacy, and to observe the limitations which it imposes upon the exercise of the authority which it gives." (Emphasis added).

A SUMMARY OF CONDITIONS SURROUNDING THIS AFFAIR

An Undisputed Record Of Good Parenting

Up until May 9, 2009, the family in this story was by all accounts and observations, a good, ROCK-SOLID family, headed by a man and woman with an UNDISPUTED record of taking good care of children. In fact, both parents had been trained and certified as foster parents. They were also screened as adoptive parents, and had cared for ten children besides their own while living in North Carolina. Their two sons had developed into outstanding young men, one becoming a Sergeant in the Marine Corps who came home and scored in the absolute top percentile of the Massachusetts State Police Exams, while the other son became a volunteer mentor of two young boys who had been growing up without the presence of their father.

The two adopted daughters of the parents pictured above were energetic, polite, multi-talented teenagers, experiencing typical pains of adolescence. Then suddenly, in the course of weeks, this seemingly great American family was broken-up, and a man's life was destroyed by people employed by state and local agencies "in order to help them." The main factors which contributed to this nightmare can be broken down into four sets of conditions;

False Allegations Based On Anger & Perceptions

The catalyst of this tragedy was the fabrication and acceptance of an incredible accusation of sexual, physical, and emotional abuse against a father of four children. The undetected falsehood, containing uncommon words and clinical phrases, some lifted off a government workplace sexual harassment poster, was skillfully laid out by an impaired and vengeful female in-law who had recently married into the family. That person is introduced and analyzed inside the chapter titled *The Executioner*.

The causal factors behind the false allegation were teenage anger and rebellion, adult anger, self-hatred, and mental illness, all of which contributed to instability and poor judgement.

A Failure To Serve & Protect

The second condition emerged because of a combination of factors, including a lack of leadership, training, and oversight, as well as misguided chivalry, political correctness, and professional negligence on the part of police.

When the false allegation was first made, police officers on duty were too eager to believe the wild tale of abuse created by three females on a quiet Sunday afternoon. In falling prey to the charm of three young women, and by not being concerned with the reputation of a man in the community, or with his Constitutional rights, officials failed to adequately question the authenticity of the false accusations being presented, and never conducted a valid investigation before bringing in outside agencies. The Department of Justice Manual on child abuse (NCJ 162425) states that "law enforcement has a legal duty and responsibility to respond accordingly," and that police "must be objective and proactive in their investigations of abuse," and "that questions of what, when, where, why, and how, must be answered."

Instead of responding with skepticism to the wild claim of abuse, which had <u>zero evidence to substantiate it,</u> and instead of <u>maintaining a professional attitude of serving and protecting</u> *a man in the community*, and instead of conducting a cautious and fair inquiry of the matter consistent with Department of Justice guidelines and other accepted professional practices, to include contacting their own chief for guidance, and instead of telephoning the parents of the children visiting the station, an officer on duty notified the Massachusetts Department of Children and Families, formerly known as the Department of Social Services.

Mandatory Reporting Laws

This action by police was partly triggered because of mandatory reporting laws. Mandatory reporting laws and mandatory sentencing guidelines always cause more problems than they solve. They always have unintended consequences. These laws have been enacted across the nation because of an atmosphere of public hysteria created by a combination of high profile crime stories, televison sensationalism, political opportunism, idiocy, and agenda-based advocacy, all of which are <u>undermining the freedom of Americans</u> and the authority of local officials to act in their rightful capacity to control and minimize minor events in their own jurisdictions.

Besides infringing on freedom, there is a large financial cost associated with mandatory reporting laws because they lead to larger government in the forms of bigger agencies, and the consumption of valuable legal system and court resources, both of which contribute to higher taxes. At same time, mandatory reporting laws lead to huge financial obligations thrown upon the citizens or families who get caught up in one type of legal tangle or another, which are most often situations which could have been quickly handled and resolved by local elders and authorities with a meeting, discussion, ticket, or a ride home (DUI). *Remember this point because it's your country, your taxes and court system, and your freedom at stake.*

Professional Malpractice

A supervisor at social services responded to the phone call from the Oxford Police, speaking briefly to both the reporting officer, and the young woman leading the false allegation. Like the officers on duty at the station, the supervisor missed an opportunity to authenticate the allegation, and uncover the hidden motive and scheme behind it. A careful review of official agency documents indicates the supervisor failed to demonstrate any concern for the parent's rights, or a man's rights, or any level of legal and moral respect for a well-established family unit, or "the sanctity of family."

Similar to police conduct during the early stages of the event, the supervisor did not respond in a cautious manner, but instead over-reacted, responding to the fantastic allegation of abuse as if there was an *actual emergency* even though no incident, injury, or evidence existed to support the wild claims being made.

The supervisor, a person assumed to possess college-level subject matter knowledge, and professional training and expertise, did not attempt, nor consider contacting the parents of the children involved with the allegation in a *good-faith effort* to gather enough information from which a *wise management decision* could be derived from. Instead, the supervisor *incited* an emergency response, dispatching not one, but TWO agents with titles of *Emergency Response Workers* to investigate the allegation on Mother's Day of 2009.

Gag Order Placed On Family, Then Father Is Exiled

The emergency workers proceeded to conduct two unwarranted entries into a private Oxford residence on Mother's Day, inspecting the living quarters and belongings of the family involved. Then, in an outrageous abuse of authority, and egregious violation of Constitution rights of citizens, agency workers placed an illegal gag order on family members, forbidding them from discussing the matter in question.

Worse yet, and again without legitimate legal authority to do so, representatives of the state ordered the accused father not to return home under threat that if he attempted to do so, his children would be taken away. Sadly, from that day forward until eternity, the father was not able to return to his home and family in his rightful place as *head of the household*. The family was subsequently broken-up and fragmented through a series of negligent and illegal actions of social service employees, police, and the courts, to such an extent, that at one point, the mother was the only person remaining at the residence in what was once a vibrant family of six members with no previous history of domestic violence or abuse.

Gross Police Negligence & Bias

A third unacceptable event occurred when police generated, then shared a criminal record check containing <u>an arrest record based on mistaken identity</u>. The arrest record they viewed and shared, and based their feelings, assumptions, and subsequent actions on was not the record of the father who had been accused of abuse, but that of another man by the same name. That man had a prior arrest record of assault and battery on a police officer, resisting arrest, and disobeying a police officer. This error is explained in greater detail in the chapters *Gross Police Negligence, and Public Servants Fail To Perform Their Duties.*

After accepting the arrest record of another man, and making it the first major supporting document to the new case file, Oxford Police, working in a spirit of cooperation with DCF workers, and individuals employed at the District Attorney's office, proceeded with an expedition of sorts to manufacture reasons to charge an innocent man with a crime against his children, and then proceeded with a *wrongful prosecution* by filing a three-count, felony criminal complaint against the father named in the allegation without sufficient probable cause, and possibly, but not confirmed, without the use and benefit of a Grand Jury. This case of <u>wrongful prosecution</u> was vigorously pursued even though (1) the father claimed his innocence in writing from the very beginning, (2) even though in the time frame of six weeks, social service workers and police neglected to conduct a legitimate investigation into conditions surrounding the allegation, and (3) even though all

11

doctors, all school counselors, and all family members stated abuse did not occur, and finally, (4) even though one of the girls involved in the allegation stepped forward to admit to the existence of a premeditated scheme involving coercion, and the creation and study of notes so that the complainant's stories would match when the trio of girls went to the police station to stage a complaint.

Facts Support The Claims Of Gross Negligence

The claim of negligence and wrongful prosecution in this case is factually supported, not only because of the father's innocence, and the erroneous police records check, but also because police and social service workers, and officials from the District Attorney's office failed to interview the two sons who lived in the home during the time-frame of the alleged abuse, and failed to speak with any *relatives or neighbors* of the girls involved, but more peculiar to *professional standards of investigation*, never interviewed Mark A. Wilmot, the person of interest, even when he contacted the chief of police for assistance.

When that recorded communication took place, the father respectfully requested help in what had become a provable *clandestine conspiracy* against him in which derogatory information was being fabricated in order to construct a criminal complaint based upon trumped-up charges. At the same time, information pointing to the father's innocence was ignored. When the father called the chief for help, the town's chief law enforcement official had a distinct opportunity, as well as a legal obligation to help a citizen in distress who had been ordered by social services that he could not return home or his children would be taken away. Through prudent action of a leader practicing oversight, the chief could have prevented a wrongful prosecution and injustice from being carried out, thus preventing un-repairable damage to people's lives.

Instead, in a manner <u>not consistent with serving and protecting</u>, the chief refused to help a father who was being misidentified and falsely accused.

Two separate legal reviews of this case have identified an astounding number of civil rights violations. Upon a legitimate review in Federal Court, the overreactions to a false allegation, the forced intrusion into an intact and functioning family, and the subsequent professional malpractice, civil rights violations, and wrongful prosecution of a bonafide American hero cannot be supported, nor condoned under strict scrutiny of the law for many reasons, beginning with the foundation of our legal system discussed in the case of Lawton v. Steel, 1893. In that established legal precedent, it clearly states "that actions of the legislative or executive branches at the state and federal level *must not violate rights and privileges* provided under the Constitution of the United States. What this means is that state government agencies cannot claim they have the power and authority under any state law, statue, or ordnance to violate the rights of any citizen, nor can state legislatures create and enact laws which violate the rights of a citizen, even when acting in such a manner might have been motivated by some noble cause such as "protecting the children."

Beside the repeated egregious violations of the family's Constitutional rights in this case, is the Commonwealth of Massachusetts' Department of Children and Families categorical failure to follow its own laws, regulations, and procedures. The obligation to do so is established case law from another precedent-setting case, DeShaney v. Winnebago County DSS, (1989): Once the state agency used force to intervene into the affairs of this Oxford family, and replaced the father with a team of social workers, the department incurred a legal responsibility to protect and nurture both minor children to insulate them from any form of harm. However, in this case both adopted daughters who had previously been trouble-free, at times became despondent teenage runaways. At other times, they were placed in lock-down protective custody, given prescription drugs against the wishes of the exiled father, and one of the daughters became an unwed, uneducated mother of two premature babies by the age of seventeen.

HOW CAN PROFESSIONALS BE BIASED AND PREJUDICED?

Forgetting The Fundamentals Of Law

The acceptance of a false allegation without supporting evidence, the amateur-like, over-reactive decision to incite an emergency response and dispatch two emergency workers with preconceived notions filling their heads, followed up by the acquisition, acceptance, and awareness of an arrest record from a misidentified person in the absence of a legitimate investigation, combined to become the foundation of erroneous facts which created an environment of extreme bias and prejudice against a good man. Once that hostile environment was created, people employed by government agencies, broke their own rules of procedure, failed to follow accepted standards of practice for law enforcement, and ignored constitutional law. At the same time, they failed to respect the privacy and best interests of an entire family unit. During the process, individuals named in this narrative took part in actions which destroyed a good family, hurt the two children they were aiming to protect, and deprived a deserving man of life, liberty, and the pursuit of his happiness.

14

How Do Preconceived Notions Affect Outcomes?

When the TWO emergency response workers from social services arrived on the scene in Oxford, they laid the groundwork for what can best be described as a hostile attack on a stable family unit. This did not occur because they are evil people, but more likely because of the culture and leadership within the system they are part of. The two investigators, also assumed to possess subject matter expertise, and professional training and knowledge, appeared to lack the capacity or willingness to fairly and accurately gather, then filter information. The reasons for this may have been because:

(1) Preconceived notions already formed in the minds of social workers on account of institutional group-think. This happens when everyone believes in the same cognitive template, and thinks in the same manner according to the group's education, training, and expectation of outcomes. This template is coupled to a frenzied, hysterical environment surrounding domestic violence and sex abuse, continually elevated because of high-profile cases, political opportunism, and television sensationalism.

(2) The field workers most likely felt obligated to substantiate the allegation of abuse, even though there was no evidence to support a finding. This occurs because of sub-optimization of institutional objectives; the agency's mission of protecting children and helping families becomes a secondary concern as a perverse underlying interest in justifying their existence and ever-growing budget takes over.

(3) Finally, the social workers could not be objective unless they were absolute professionals in possession of a concern for family rights, and a man's rights. This would have insulated them from the erroneous, false, biased, and unsubstantiated information they were receiving by cell phone as they drove to a small town to investigate a dubious claim that ten years of mental, physical, and sexual abuse had been committed against two teenage girls.

THE STATE-SPONSORED TERRORISM BEGINS

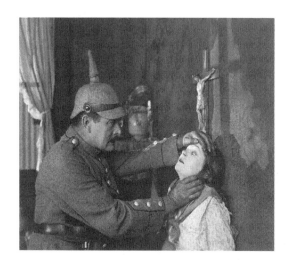

Two Men Arrive Unexpectedly At A Home

Early in the evening on Mother's Day 2009, two investigators, each assigned the title of *Emergency Response Worker*, employed by the *Massachusetts Department of Children and Families*, arrived at a townhouse located at 21-2 Thayer Pond Drive, in North Oxford, Massachusetts. A few hours earlier, at 12:42, a female relative of the family, who had been temporarily living at the same address, escorted two teenage girls to the Oxford Police Station. Once inside, the relative explained to the police officer at the window that she wanted to file a report of child abuse. The three females were invited inside the station where the overly-concerned relative could elaborate.

After speaking with Sergeant Michael Hasset, an officer who would later be named as the new chief by town officials, the relative spent about thirty minutes constructing an exceptionally well-written statement which *attempted* to describe ten years of

16

mental, physical, and sexual abuse against the two teenage girls in her company. The neatly written statement lacked evidence of specific incidents, but was noteworthy in its wide scope, containing textbook descriptions of each category of abuse. There were no incidents, actions, reports of injuries, or related matter to make reference to, even though the allegation was promoting a claim that ten years of total abuse had been carried out against two young girls.

During the initial interviews, according to police reports, one child stated that she was never hit by her father, and that there was "no penetration," while the younger child never described being struck, spanked, or hit, and never claimed to have been sexually assaulted by her father. Despite these contrary expressions, the written statement provided by the relative cleverly incriminated the girls' adoptive father while portraying a terrible home life for the two teenagers.

After speaking briefly with all three girls, Sergeant Hassett of the Oxford Police made a decision to call the "Judge Baker" child abuse hotline. He came into contact with Justine Tonelli, a supervisor at the Department of Children and Families. Ms. Tonelli conferred with the officer, then spoke with the complaining relative, who volunteered "*to take the children*."

What Constitutes An Emergency?

At this point, the supervisor made a decision to *incite* and activate an emergency response, and dispatched two *Emergency Response Workers*, Kevin Foley and Michael Polinski, out to the town of Oxford to *investigate* the matter.

When the supervisor made her decision to incite an emergency response, there was no evidence that any abuse occurred – there was simply an allegation being made by three calm young ladies who were physically and emotionally well, bearing no evidence of injury or assault. However, the allegation that more than ten years of sexual, physical, and mental abuse had taken place at the hands of the girls' father attracted everyone's attention, stirring up a lynch-mob mentality *to go get the perpetrator*.

The fact is that when the decision to activate an emergency response was made by Justine Tonelli, no real emergency existed. If an emergency condition did not exist, subsequent actions by the state employees could not pass what is known in legal circles as the *strict scrutiny test.*

If an emergency condition had actually existed that Sunday afternoon, then perhaps there might be *sufficient cause* to allow local and state employees to claim they had a compelling interest, and therefore a legitimate reason to take all means necessary to forcefully intervene into a family unit such as the Wilmot family. However, that was clearly not the case. What factually existed on May 10, 2009 was a well-written allegation – a wild fabrication of storybook proportions, far from the truth, authored by an unstable relative of two rebellious girls whom she had brought to the police station.

In The Absence of Professional Scrutiny . . .

In the absence of professional scrutiny and good judgement, and without the benefit of a *cautious and fair inquiry*, the fabricated *storyline* became effective enough to trigger a manhunt of sorts. What is meant by that? Because of conditions in society, and because of political correctness and idiocy, agencies quickly embarked on an expedition to hunt down "the perpetrator," and quickly convict him of abuse. At the same time, their mind-set was geared toward turning the two young children at the police station into victims of imaginary crimes which sometimes only exist in the minds of people who believe they were once wronged themselves, or by people who are professionally ignorant, or by those that earn their money in the arena of child-protective services, and therefore have a predisposition to believe society is full of "abusers."

OPERATING UNDER THE COLOR OF THE LAW

Theresa Wilmot, a mother, was approached without warning at her front door by two male DCF investigators on Mother's Day

A Professional's Frame Of Reference

It's difficult to know for sure, however, it's likely that two crucial frames of reference were not structuring the thoughts of police or social service workers during the early stages of this event. The first missing frame of reference was the *desire to serve* the community as servants; i.e., by viewing oneself as a service provider, and by viewing the father and mother, and family they were about to visit as customers, or "end-users" of the service they provide.

The second frame of reference was a keen awareness of a well-known legal principle that all men are presumed innocent until proven guilty via the presentation of evidence in court.

This principle is _real law_. Enforcement of this law lies at the very foundation of the administration of our legal system. The principle was upheld and is accepted case law stemming from the case of Coffin v. United States, 156 U.S. 432 (1895). What it means is that if all men (citizens) are innocent until proven guilty with supporting evidence presented in a court of law, then representatives of state and local government cannot punish a man based on an allegation. Most unfortunately, that is exactly what was about to happen to Mark A. Wilmot of North Oxford, a retired Marine, a certified foster parent, and a screened adoptive parent who introduces himself in the chapter titled, _Meet The Accused._

What Was Their Objective During This Home Visit?

When the two social service investigators interviewed the three girls at the police station, all three repeated an eerily similar story that more than ten years of abuse had taken place at the hands of the teenagers' father who was being portrayed as a real monster of a human being.

☆After the second interview of the girls was completed, at which point the complaining relative again offered to "_take the girls_," the two investigators drove over to the girls' residence at Thayer Pond Village to conduct what should have been a cautious and fair inquiry into allegations of child abuse.

Again, it must be referenced that several important frames of reference and intent were not present at this time. The visit to the targeted home had already become a mission to confirm a suspicion, rather than to conduct a fair inquiry. A desire to minimize the abuse claims, and to leave a family alone to conduct their own affairs did not exist in their minds. _The men were not sensitive to the potential impact of their intrusion into the sanctity (sacredness) of a family._ All the emergency workers had to accomplish during this home visit was to act under the color of the law, utilize their tool box of authority and dirty tricks which had become polished through repetition of their job duties, and their preconceived notions, based on institutional immersion and group-think, would instantly become true.

✶After locating a vacant parking space near the home at Thayer Pond Village, the two men ambushed the unsuspecting mother of the two minor girls as the mother stood outside her home. Using the power of the state, and acting under the color of the law, the men coyly and without warrant, gained entry to the three-level townhouse occupied by the Wilmot Family.

Under close scrutiny, this action violated the Fourth Amendment constitutional right of the Wilmot family, i.e., through the act of conducting an entry and unreasonable search without warrant, which occurs in many different forms according to past court rulings.

After examining the rooms and contents of the home, and interrogating the mother, the two men departed, then returned again later in the evening and re-entered the home through use of authority, again without a search warrant.

An Intrusion Into Family Privacy

Mark A. Wilmot, the father of the girls whom it is alleged that he abused, and the head of the household, was not home at the time of the intrusion, as he was painting a room for his mother as a Mother's Day gift. Because of the absence of an authority figure at the home, the agents immediately established the upper hand as they began waging an unwarranted and unjust campaign of terror upon a completely unsuspecting American family.

During their two intrusions into the sanctity of the Wilmot residence, the men questioned the mother about the children's room, the door to the room, about the why the father told his daughters to take showers, and why the father brought his children to buy bathing suits at Sears each year.

An Oxford police officer also entered the home sometime during the evening, joining with the two social service agents in creating an intimidating environment in the otherwise peaceful Wilmot home.

Review What Has Happened So Far

At this early stage, let's review what has happened so far; an allegation of abuse has been made against a man, a father of four. Police did not question conditions surrounding the allegation, and a social service supervisor has *converte*d the allegation into an emergency condition, and *incited* an emergency response.

Two emergency response workers are ordered to the scene. Using power and coy tricks gained from previous experiences, they arrive in force at a private residence, on a day of worship, and on a family holiday. Without warning, they confront a woman who is a mother of four children as she stands in front of the entrance to her home. The two men demand access under authority of color of the law. The woman, who is taken by complete surprise, is incapable of defending herself or her home in such a situation, so the two men succeed in making forced entry into a private residence, "a home of an American," on the sole basis of an allegation which was made without any evidence to support it.

✶The facts at this stage in this story are that no crime had been committed, and no factual emergency existed. The agents of the government, i.e., police and social service workers, had no legal basis to invade, inspect, and assume control over the residence of an American without a search warrant based on reasonable and probable cause. The sudden visit to the Wilmot's well-kept home, carried out on a family holiday by government agents, was in fact the beginning of a criminal probe. The two men would gather information which would later be used to make a "discretionary referral" to the District Attorney for criminal prosecution of the head of the Wilmot family. Theresa Wilmot, an American citizen, the caring mother of the two girls who had been brought to the police station, having no knowledge of the origins or cause of the situation, and outnumbered by the surprise posse comitatus, is not cognizant of the gravity of the affair as it quickly unfolded, nor was she mentally prepared, or intellectually and physically capable of taking the necessary measures to protect her family unit.

The social service workers forcing their way into the Wilmot's residence, with back-up from an armed police officer, are accustomed to a condition in which they are never rightfully challenged by uniformed citizens whom they typically encounter. These public servants, *creatures of the law, who are legally bound to obey and to observe the limitations imposed upon the exercise of that authority,* saw no need to proceed with caution, to simply drop off a brochure, offer services, talk with neighbors, or invite the parents of the girls to call the agency the following business day to discuss a developing concern related to the wild allegations constructed that day.

The truth of the matter is that law enforcement and social service workers did not follow agency regulations, rules, and accepted standards of practices. Nor did they advise, or recommend that the mother have an attorney present before she responded to their questions, or subjected her home to their inspection. Within the next chapters, you are going to learn what the public servants did once they got inside the Wilmot home. What you are about to learn is not only despicable, but it represents an egregious violation of the Constitutional rights of each of the family members.

Supreme Court Justice James Marshall wrote in Marbury v. Madison, "the phraseology of the Constitution confirms and strengthens the principle supposed to be essential to all constitutions, that any law repugnant to the Constitution is void, and that courts, as well as other departments are bound by that instrument" (1803)

A SON COMES HOME TO STRANGERS IN HIS HOUSE

The Sanctity Of A Home

Preston Wilmot, the twenty-four-year-old son of Mark and Theresa Wilmot, returned to his home on Sunday evening of Mother's Day, to find strangers inside his home. Before he stepped inside his house, he approached the driveway, walking past a small car on the street. That car belonged to his brother's new wife, Michelle. She is the relative who had escorted his two younger sisters to the police station earlier that day, where she wrote the statement containing allegations of abuse. Michelle is also the person, who at this early stage of the affair, has already offered three times, "*to take the girls*."

Preston observed Michelle inside her car, in the driver's seat. Davalia, his younger sister, sat in the front passenger seat next to Michelle. What he did not know at the time is that Michelle was instructing Davalia to keep her eyes fixed on her, and not to acknowledge Preston in any manner. Preston tapped on the car window, but both occupants ignored him, so he went inside his home.

The Coercion Of A Child

✶Thirteen-year-old Davalia Wilmot, the youngest of the Wilmot children, would later reveal that she already knew what she was doing was wrong because her father had not abused her or her sister. Less than one month after the Mother's Day allegation, Davalia would write a letter to the District Attorney in which she recanted her allegations of abuse made during the multi-person plot to get back at, or get away from the control of her parents. During the following months, Davalia had the courage to provide first-hand source material about what really transpired. When combined with official agency documents, eyewitness accounts, and the findings of the author's investigation, Davalia's revelations helped make this book the most accurate portrayal of *what really happened.*

Inside the car that evening, Davalia was crying, already wanting to reverse the course of events. However, Michelle, the wife of Donald Wilmot, who is the oldest child of Mark and Theresa Wilmot, was hellbent on keeping a manipulative grip over Davalia by preventing her from speaking up, while at the same time reinforcing the notion that she and her sister had been abused for most of their life.

Sensing that something was drastically wrong, Preston cautiously entered his home through the front door. He walked upstairs, passing a policeman standing near the top landing. He witnessed the other two aggressively-postured men inside the Wilmot home as he took a seat at the dining room table where the family normally gathered for well-rounded meals and conversation. Preston observed Kandice, his other younger sister having a temper tantrum whereas she was stomping her feet on the floor while saying she did not feel safe in the house, and saying she wanted to leave. Preston did not understand why Kandice was *acting* in this manner.

Unreasonable Search and Abuse of Power

What Preston walked into at his home was an unexpected, and *unwarranted* search, *investigation*, and *intrusive action* by government agents into a private residence in the town of North Oxford, the state of Massachusetts, and the country of the United States of America, a Nation which takes pride in its tradition of individual freedom and liberty for all. Before moving on, consider what the Fourth Amendment to the Constitutional guarantees all Americans:

*The right of the people to be secure in their persons, houses, papers, and effects, **against unreasonable searches** and seizures, shall not be violated, and no warrant shall issue, but upon probable cause, supported by Oath or affirmation, and particularly describing the place to be searched, and the persons or things to be seized.*

Court Precedents Create Established Case Law

Two court precedents affirmed the Fourth Amendment right of every family to have protection from unreasonable searches and seizures by social service workers. In both cases, the U. S. Ninth Circuit Court of Appeals found that Child Protective Services' entry into a home when there is no emergency or without a warrant are violations of the parents' Fourth Amendment rights.

The first case, Calabretta v. Floyd, involved a county social worker, accompanied by a police officer, forced entry into the Calabretta home without a warrant. Social workers are bound to obey the U.S. Constitution when investigating child abuse cases. With respect to the Fourth Amendment, the Ninth Circuit settled the question once and for all saying that no longer can any social worker enter a home without either a warrant or probable cause of an emergency.

In a second case, social workers in Escondido, California, and local police seized two children from a home in the middle of the night, without a warrant. The seizure was based on a tip from a family member. Three days later, the children were examined at a hospital without their parents present. Despite finding no evidence of abuse, the children were kept from their parents for more than two months. The court ruled that a jury should decide whether the city of Escondido had a policy of picking up children without verifying the existence of a court order and without reasonable cause.

✱ With this decision, the Ninth Circuit opened the way for the family to sue for "damages on the allegations of civil rights violations, abduction of the children and infliction of emotional distress.

ON MOTHER'S DAY?

Theresa read to her daughters, even as they get older

A Casual Neglect of Constitutional Law & Case Law

The official purpose for the intimidating visit to the Wilmot home on Sunday, May 10, 2009, Mothers Day, was so the emergency response workers could inspect the premises, and "interrogate" the parents inside the townhouse to "investigate" allegations of child abuse. Just think about this action; in the absence of any evidence of a physical injury, a sex act, or a criminal act, but on the thin excuse made possible by a wild allegation made that day, should social workers, with a police escort, have visited this home on Mother's Day, or any other home for that matter, or was it an instance of overzealousness, poor judgment, and a lack of training and supervisory oversight of the public servants involved?

Perhaps the most important point regarding the Mother's Day intrusion into the Wilmot family is that agents and police were *casual in their neglect* of the Bills of Rights, while they were zestfully deliberate in their effort *to get the perpetrator*.

This mode of operation is a provable pattern of behavior by the Department of Social Services but should never be accepted by the public because it is an assault on freedom.

The agents in this story, and their supervisor, perceived no need to postpone the investigation until the following day when both parents, and an attorney could meet to discuss details of the matter.

✷The fact of the matter is that the intrusion into the Wilmot home on Mother's Day, and the inspection of the belongings, and the questioning of its occupants, was a violation of the Wilmot's constitutional rights, because in America, the citizenry has a reasonable right to privacy in their home, while at the same time, the government does not enjoy the authority to conduct an unwarranted visit, or "search and inspection" of a private residence despite the agents' belief that such authority exists in state laws.

Later on in this story, a lawyer working for the Department of Children and Families will express this same sentiment, telling Mark A. Wilmot, the father of the Wilmot family, that Constitutional Law does not apply to employees and actions of the Department of Children and Families.

MEET THE ABUSED

**Before this wonderful child was adopted by Mark
and Terry Wilmot, she lived in three other home settings**

Adopted Children Facing Turbulence and Instability

The two girls whom a relative accused the father of abusing for
a period of ten years, first came to the Wilmot family during 1996.
Prior to that, they lived at another foster home in Jacksonville,
North Carolina. The two sisters were eventually adopted by Mark
and Terry Wilmot, but that occurred after they left the Wilmot
home because they were adopted by their biological grandparents.
That adoption failed, so the children came back to the Wilmot
family as foster children a second time. So, in the course of their
first years, the two girls you are about to learn more about lived in
four different home settings, with four different sets of
circumstances affecting their development.

Kandice on her first night in the Wilmot home

Normal early childhood developmental did not occur because of the unusual instability, as well as other factors related to habits and lifestyles of the biological parents. Kandice and Davalia came from a family of eight. All the children in that original family were in jeopardy because of what was occurring within the family unit. Two of their older siblings became emotionally disturbed because of the North Carolina situation. Kandice was headed down the same path when intervention by social services occurred. As a toddler, Kandice received speech therapy in the Wilmot home by a trained professional in order to help her learn to communicate. A depressed element of personality, and the cognitive delay remained with her, causing a very slight impediment which only became evident to alert observers during certain activities. As a child, Kandice's outward appearance often included dark circles under her eyes. She demonstrated a slight disability in speech development and cognitive reaction time. While sleeping, she did so in an unusual twisted position. While watching television, no matter what program, she became distant, and wept slow, silent tears. As she grew older, she experienced angry outbursts, and instances of questionable integrity, but all her conditions steadily improved with age, especially with the absolute love, nurture, guidance, and effort expended by her parents, who were committed to helping Kandice develop into a smart, strong, good person.

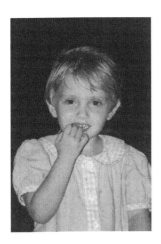

The lingering effects of an unstable beginning

Michelle, the visiting sister-in-law, developed a fondness of both girls, and observed, then misinterpreted Kandice's pre-existing conditions and teenage complaints to imply she was being abused by her adoptive father. Subsequently, because of Michelle's negative life experiences, and destructive disposition toward others, especially men, she attempted to become both a savior and vengeful executioner against the girls' adoptive father by hatching a scheme to gain custody of the girls. This reality was obvious from the beginning of the episode.

Davalia (pictured below) was also profoundly affected by the instability of her biological family's situation as she was literally born into extreme turmoil. She displayed rage, frustration, and physical withdrawal, causing her to act out in a manner not worthy of describing. Davalia also had an extraordinary appetite, sometimes consuming up to fifteen large bottles of baby formula in a single day. The Wilmot family, including Donald and Preston, worked hard at helping Davalia overcome her physical and emotional frustrations by meeting her emotional and physical needs.

Of factual relevance to what transpired in this story, is that a series of unusual events happened to both girls during early childhood. An undisclosed set of circumstances led to the termination of the first adoption by their grandparents, and their return to foster care. Keep in mind that these events occurred after their biological parents' rights had been terminated, and also after they had been in two different foster homes. Despite their rough start in life, my wife Terry and I, and our two sons, Donald and

Preston, and the extended family, welcomed Kandice and Davalia into the Wilmot family where they were given an *extraordinary* amount of love and nurturing.

The Facts Are Certain

The facts mentioned concerning the girls' early years are certain. I mentioned this over the phone to the investigators on Mother's Day, when the lawyer told me not to meet with them until he could be present. Feeling obligated to find evidence of some type of abuse, they did not care to listen, nor did they consider the possibility there might be more to the abuse allegation then what they had heard and read to this point, and what their organizational culture led them to *assume*. It must be stressed that they possessed a certain motivation to arrive at a finding which met institutional expectations, while at the same time they were not motivated by thoughts of parents' rights, respect for the family unit, or reverence for the Constitution.

Another fact is what did not happen in subsequent years as the girls grew older in the Wilmot home; they were not mentally, physically, or sexually abused. My wife and I considered Kandice and Davalia miracles in our lives, gifts from God, to be taken care of. We loved them as much, if not more than any parent loves a natural-born child.

Speaking for myself, I was one-hundred percent *committed* to protecting, nurturing, and teaching Kandice and Davalia as much as possible before they would go out into the world to fend for themselves. The pages of this book contain pictures taken over the years. These pictures clearly illustrate the type of relationship my wife and I had with Kandice and Davalia, and the kind of life they lived. The relationship we all shared in the Wilmot family was physically and mentally close, without a single indicator that something was wrong or abusive.

As a father, and adoptive parent, I did my personal best to provide each girl with all the tools needed to succeed in life, never abusing them along the way. I was their number one guardian and teacher, their best asset in life. My wife and I both did our best to help Kandice and Davalia become exceptionally good people, just like our two sons. For these reasons, this episode of false allegations, followed up by wantonly reckless state intervention into our lives, is that much more painful to me, my wife, and all the relatives who contributed to improving the girl's lives.

A foster parent shows his children how to slide

MEET THE ACCUSED

Master Sergeant Mark A. Wilmot, USMC (ret.)

Would You Trust This Man With Your Life?

This chapter provides information which conveys how a father whose family was taken away by public servants, spent the majority of his life striving to be a good son, a good man, a good father, and a good American. This biographical information, and the author's opinions are important because they will help readers begin to fathom just how much personal *honor* and liberty has been stolen from a decent man who could be viewed as a traditional American man. Once you finish reading this chapter, and the next, you will have a grasp of the tremendous disconnect between reality of a person's character vs. developed perception of an abuser.

Is Government Operating Where It Does Not Belong?

To begin with, let me say this; I am an American citizen who strongly objects to the violation of his constitutional rights, the destruction of his family by government forces, and on a larger scale, the loss of any freedoms or liberty of any American. By the time you finish this chapter, you will better understand why I'm a freedom fighter who must come out of military retirement to fight a new battle, this time not against a foreign enemy, but against a domestic one instead. That domestic enemy is the idiotic and corrupt system of government intervention into the private affairs of good families, and the trend in which the government is inserting itself into the business of everything Americans do as *free* people, i.e., this is all about the ongoing loss of freedom.

What is happening in America regarding the meddling into the private affairs of citizens is *illegal according to our basic system of law*. For example, if you were to renew your knowledge of the Constitution, the legal framework of the nation, you will not be able to locate any legal basis for the establishment and funding of so-called family support agencies, or health care plans for that matter. On the other hand, you will find reference to the raising of taxes to support a standing army for the defense of the nation. With that stated, the government should not be operating in other areas of our lives to the extent it is, unless it is *absolutely* necessary for the welfare or security of the country. The government does not belong in your house, or in your refrigerator, or in your doctor's office. You should strive to keep them out of these areas, and out of your life whenever possible. The reason the government has become entangled in the business of interfering with families, and encroaching more and more on individual rights is a direct result of idiocy, and the fact that more and more people are becoming ignorant to the fact that more government means less freedom. With that stated, let me tell you a little about my life, which began during 1959.

Developing An Appreciation For Freedom

Over fifty years ago, I was an innocent, skinny child, number seven in line, from a low-income, Catholic, church-going family consisting of five sisters, three brothers, a mother, and a father. We lived on the edge of a small town, in a five-room house was built from a few boards, tiles, stones, and buckets of cement every weekend by my father, who was assisted by family and friends. Back then, it was not that difficult to build your own home because the government was not overly-involved in the process (if they even were involved at all). The modern burden of residential regulations and taxation on the home owner had not yet become the barrier to home-building that it is today. My father could not build a home today like he did back then, because the local government inspector, and probably an environmentalist would stop him. This illustrates how the creation of regulations and laws works to restrict freedom. At the same time, this example also illustrates how the perceived need for enforcement of a rule, regulation, or law, creates a further need of taxation to pay the salaries of public servants who will get paid to restrict your freedom.

Additional laws and regulations always translate into bigger government, higher taxes, and less individual freedom. As a child, I didn't understand the correlation between freedom, liberty, and big government. I do now. Back then, I was just a free-running boy who went fishing, and who attended the Memorial Day parade with his friends to watch veterans of the two big world wars march by, and to listen to the receding of the great Gettysburg address, given to us by Abraham Lincoln.

Like many other men before me, I learned how to shoot and hunt at the North Worcester Fox & Coon Club. Yes, it's true, I was one of those types being raised to believe in shooting guns, and defending the concepts of life, liberty, and the pursuit of happiness, things which many of us celebrate every Fourth of July which is the celebration of *Independence Day*.

So maybe it's not surprising that I grew up to be a United States Marine, capable of shooting a variety of weapons, effectively hitting targets up to a thousand yards away.

Like building a home, shooting a weapon as I did as a child would be much more difficult today. The reason is because, once again, the government has grown bigger, and more laws have been passed to restrict gun ownership and gun possession, making it more difficult for Americans to be free as we were intended to be free by our founding fathers. Keep this reality mind; when guns are completely outlawed, only outlaws and the police will have guns. This will leave regular people like you and me in a very difficult, and defenseless position if the government goes bad, and especially if the police don't care about the Constitution, or if they are corrupt, ignorant, or overzealous.

A Hometown Boy Becomes A Champion

I have to admit it; by the time I arrived in high school, I was a failed student, but I was not an idiot. I had a great intellect but it just did not happen for me in the classroom. I did pretty well outside the classroom as a distance runner, winning two cross country championships, and the New England AAU one-mile, and 3,000 meter steeplechase championships. That means I became a winner and a champion at a young age, something that not everyone gets to experience, even once in their lifetime. Despite this, I remained an uninspired scholar, however, before graduating, I did manage to pass four years of Latin, become president of the Varsity Club, and get voted "Most Athletic."

A year after graduation, after not surviving on a college campus, I enlisted in the United States Marine Corps. Upon completion of basic training at Paris Island, South Carolina, and eleven months of training in Tennessee and California, I volunteered to be screened, and was subsequently *selected* to serve with the President's Helicopter Squadron. This selection occurred after passing the rigorous standards which would allow the granting of a secret-security clearance. I was then stationed at the president's helicopter facility located in Quantico, Virginia during the Carter and Reagan presidencies. During that time, I qualified for an opportunity to compete on the All-Marine collegiate track team, running the mile and the relay.

In subsequent years, I reenlisted several times. As a reward, the Marine Corps and Navy provided thousands of hours of additional training and education. I was able to travel the world, and serve in many different command and leadership capacities. I often volunteering for tough missions, and the missions nobody else really wanted to do. I eventually earned a promotion to the staff noncommissioned officer rank of *Master Sergeant.* While attending a senior-level leadership school, I became an honor graduate, and received the *Sergeant Major of The Marine Corps Leadership Writing Award* for writing a winning thesis on the subject of making a difference in people's lives, on and off the military base.

I remained a highly-dedicated, and effective Marine and leader of men until the Commandant placed me on the *fully-retired* list during 2008, thirty-years after I first enlisted into the Corps.

Who Am I Today?

As I record events inside this book, I'm a middle-aged local man who once lived in North Oxford, Massachusetts. I don't live there now because I've been forced into exile. I'm not just any man, not a perfect man by any means, but a good man, who is in the fight of his life because the local District Attorney's office is processing criminal charges against me for child abuse. These charges stem from fabrications, bias, and prejudice, plus the gross negligence of the local police department, and the Department of Children and Families, but also a result of both agencies conspiring to deprive me of my constitutional rights while they went about destroying my family and ruining my life.

During my adult years, I made it a habit to actively seek knowledge and understand life, but I have to say there is no way to completely understand, nor accept what has happened to my family. However, if there is someone who can put the story down on paper for others to read about, it would be me. The reason is because I taught myself how to write, then publish books, starting with the elementary steps of the binding process, which I learned to accomplish by hand just as monks did hundreds of years ago. As years went by, I developed an interest in life story writing for the purpose of preserving the memories of those who died before their time was up.

After helping several people record their life stories, I wrote and published several titles of my own, including *Capturing The Essence of Life, Redemption of A Street Fighter*, and *Sharing Your Life Story In The Digital Age*.

Redemption of A Street Fighter is a paper book used by myself and my good friend Louis Mejia to save lives, and provide spiritual hope and inspiration to people, especially people *on the street.*

Ironically, one of the last book projects I was developing inside my home office located inside the garage, prior to being forced away from my home by the Department of Children and Families, is titled *Can I Become A Good Man.* It's a book, which when finished, will help young teenagers and young men find their way to being a good man in the absence of positive examples to emulate. How ironic is that?

Besides learning how to write books, I also created a whole new indoor/outdoor sport in order to help fight childhood obesity, and to provide more children with an opportunity to play a team sport. To embark on such a project, which came forth from a drawing on a napkin, and then became a reality through inspired hard work, I had to be a person with absolute courage and inner strength.

What Kind Of Neighbor?

What is it like to know me as a neighbor and friend? Let me just say that I make *every attempt* to be a good man, and taken a step further, I make *every attempt* to be there for anyone who needs a hand. I'm the type of guy who honors his mother and father, and a man who waits and opens doors for the elderly.

You know what I'm saying – I'm the type of guy who stops along the freeway to help strangers when their vehicle is disabled in the middle of nowhere. I'm the type of guy that volunteers to give classes to community organizations like the boy scouts and girl scouts. I'm also the type of man who gives a few dollars to people on the streets, even when others say one shouldn't encourage panhandling bums, and other lost souls. Last, but not least, I donate my resources and time and thousands of copies of *Redemption of A Street Fighter*, to give hope and salvation to people in need of hope. I go about these charity works, not for recognition and acclaim, but because of what I have become.

Because of my core values and beliefs, I am the man who takes certain actions without thinking twice. For example, I'm the man who received a commendation medal for heroic achievement for stopping a major crime on a city street, while assisting police at the same time. Actions such as that are personal actions which I undertook not just once, but many times during my lifetime. In the final analysis, I am what I am – a real man, a custodian of his family, and his country, who has a solidified belief system based on three things; (1) traditions of the Catholic church, (2) Marine Corps core values; honor, courage, commitment, honoring fellow Marines, the country, and the family, (3) the Constitution and the Declaration of Independence.

Taking The Oath Seriously

In all reality, I am a man with courage and wisdom. While not considered educated or highly credentialed by typical standards, I'm an intellectual with the brain power, wisdom, and experience to back it up. I'm also a man who appreciates the importance of the Fourth of July, a man who carries the Marine Corps' core values card in his wallet, and a man that stands-by his responsibility to uphold the oath which he swore to as a Marine. That oath contains the meaningful phrase *"to protect the country against all enemies, both foreign and domestic."*

Yes, I take the oath seriously.

With that oath in mind, I am a man concerned for the future of America, and a man who can spot a communist or a socialist, or their useful idiots a mile away. I can see through their folly, and the falseness of it all. That's why I am a man opposed to higher taxes which support government activities which serve to restrict freedom. Even though I'm no longer in uniform, I remain deeply concerned because there really are enemies, both within, and outside the country's borders. One of those internal enemies is characterized by the traits of ignorance and idiocy. You will come to know that enemy well as you read further into this book.

Mark Wilmot is shown receiving a medal for heroic achievement

WHAT KIND OF FATHER?

Mark, Donald, and Preston Wilmot

Two More Good Men Come Forth

This chapter conveys what kind of father I was before the Oxford police, and employees of the Department of Children and Families conspired to separate me from my family and residence, and replace me with a team of social workers.

My life as a father begins with the arrival of two sons, whom I am so proud to stand next to, and call my own. I am the man who raised one of these sons to have the courage and strength to volunteer to serve his country during wartime. This son named Donald, traveled to the combat zone, then back again three times, becoming an outstanding sergeant in the Marine Corps along the way. Today, he performs special work for the country.

It's also true that I am the man who raised another outstanding son, named Preston, who has honor and conviction, who became a solid man, and dedicated youth mentor at the age of twenty-two.

Preston mentors not just one, but two young boys who are growing up in a nearby city without a father in their life. Both of the Wilmot sons are good men. Anyone would be fortunate to have these two men as a neighbor or a friend.

A significant factor contributing to their status as good men, and their capacity to be such, is the fact that I did my best to teach them to be that way. Perhaps this is a fitting place to share a poem that Preston wrote during his teenage years:

Dad Is A Piece of Gold In A Cave of Bronze

When Dad wakes me,

he does it like the gentle break of a wave.

When he talks to me,

he is stern but caring, like a father wolf.

He lights a fire to get the job done.

He is the influence of my life.

He is the guard of the family,

always on duty, never willing to stop

To know Dad is there, is very comforting.

He is the most special person I know.

Dad is a piece of gold in a cave of bronze

Like his father, and like his brother Don, Preston developed into a winner – a solid example of a good man – smart, strong, and a good person. He also volunteered to become a mentor to not just one, but two fatherless boys from Worcester

Mark is shown pushing Davalia on the swing-set during
a summer 2008 trip to Uncle Bill and Aunt Karen's
vacation home located in Narragansett, Rhode Island

Besides raising two fine sons, I am also a father who volunteered, along with his wife, to take care of not just one or two, but ten foster children. These foster children included babies hurt by parents' substance-abuse, failure-to-thrive babies, and children living in garbage-strewn, cockroach-infested environments. I took care of, and nurtured those needy children during my spare time, *while serving on active duty in the Marines.*

I am also the father who adopted two young girls who had been foster children in Jacksonville, North Carolina. They were first adopted by their biological grandparents, but incidents occurred which caused that adoption to fail, at which time my wife and I were asked if we wanted to have the girls return to our home. I am the father who taught these two young adopted girls, whom I considered miracles in my life, everything from gardening to shooting, from reading to writing, from swimming to running like a champion, from cooking a turkey, to deboning a chicken after it has been served, from rolling meatballs to making spaghetti, from cutting and dicing peppers, onions, and garlic to make fresh chili, from mixing and rolling egg rolls, to serving a great family dinner. I am the father who encouraged them to learn how to sing, act, and play musical instruments. I am the man who sought to help them understand political issues, and the big picture of life, yes I was teaching them about freedom. I loved these girls as much as any parent could love their own biological children, and I placed great effort into their lives. What is most important, I am the man who strived to have these children grow up to be well-rounded, smart, strong, Christian people.

Besides encouraging his children to be smart, strong, and good people, Mark also encouraged them to be physically fit

A Man Who Is Forced Away From His Own Home

Last but not least, I am the father who was forced away from his family, home, and life's work on Mother's Day, 2009, simply because a relative harboring deep resentment and distorted perspectives toward men, fabricated malicious allegations of abuse, and then convinced two angry teenagers to go along with the plot. Instead of being fair, cautious, and professional, public servants jumped at the opportunity to interfere in a family, following a predetermined script created by idiocy, which presumes guilt, and demands destructive intervention contrary to their own goals of helping families. So, my last note of claim to fame is that I am, or I was, the head of the household, a soon-to-be patriarch of a good family that was destroyed by the Massachusetts Department of Children and Families, incompetency of town police officers, and the forces of idiocy flourishing within the social services industry and society.

Davalia dances with her father at the annual Father-Daughter Dance held at the middle school

MARCHING TO THE GAS CHAMBER

Why It's Important To Question Authority

☆It was at the family table, in the family living room, that members of the Wilmot family were issued an unlawful gag order, by agents Kevin Foley and/or Michael Polenski, that forbade them, or anyone else, from discussing the details of what was occurring. Not knowing any better, and feeling intimidated by the state and local agents serving in roles as public servants, the Wilmot's fell right in line, as if they were prisoners during World War II, marching to a gas chamber with the mistaken belief they would be given a hot shower. This unlawful gag order by people acting on behalf of the state, kept the Wilmot parents uninformed, legally vulnerable, and defenseless for more than six weeks as an unfounded, false allegation accelerated out of control, becoming a full-fledged criminal complaint against Mark Wilmot, the head of the household.

★★★Official agency records show that by June 10, 2009, one full month after the substandard investigation began, Sergeant Green notified social service case worker Tara Tracy that he would be charging Mark Wilmot with felony indecent assault, and assault and battery against his daughters. When this decision to request a warrant for the arrest of Mark Wilmot was made by the Oxford police, Mr. and Mrs. Wilmot still had no indication of what they were up against, meaning their Fifth and Sixth Amendment Rights were clearly being violated.

Another aspect to keep in mind while all of this is occurring is this; during this one-month time frame, all of the public servants involved in this case of gross injustice worked their jobs each day, and each of them was able to return home to see their families each night, and to enjoy liberty. However, Mark A. Wilmot, a real life decorated hero, and head of a great American family living in Oxford, Massachusetts, is devastated and isolated, not able to return home to his family, work, or personal possessions because, through the issuance of an illegal order by the investigating social service workers, he has been told that his children will be taken away if he returns home.

The Fifth Amendment to the Constitution says;

"No person shall be held to answer for a capital or otherwise infamous crime, unless on the presentment of a grand jury, except in cases arising in the land or naval forces, or in the militia, when in actual service in time of war or public danger; nor shall any person be subject for the same offense to be twice put in jeopardy of life or limb, nor shall be compelled in any criminal case to be a witness against himself, nor be deprived of life, liberty, or property, without due process of law; nor shall private property be taken for public use without compensation."

During the period of early May through June, the Wilmot family is becoming more and more confused, and is beginning to disintegrate under the intense pressure of the situation. Sadly, the Wilmot family has become just another case, an administrative file to be dealt with only when a question arises from an outside source, or when a procedural action, such as a review meeting is required.

In Massachusetts, more than sixty-thousand allegations of abuse are reported each year. More than four-thousand of those allegations become cases just like the Wilmot case. This helps the Department of Children and Families justify its huge budget of hundreds of millions of dollars. It also helps the department get more funding, sometimes reported to be more than one-hundred and fifty-thousand dollars for every new case opened.

After considering the performance of the social workers in this story, which is explained in one of the final chapters, you could justifiably become deeply concerned about the large number of cases opened each year, not just in Massachusetts, but in other states as well. In the author's opinion, and in the author's experience, the large numbers clearly indicate the government is out of control, and interfering in families where it does not belong.

As the man whose family and life were destroyed by the actions of the public servants and agencies involved, it's my position that no government agency, regardless of how well- intentioned it might be, can replace the love and nurture of two parents in the life of a child. I will prove that position while writing this book. *Families and parents do have rights.* When considering the family unit, the basic economic unit of the nation, the connection between parents and their children is a natural relationship, with natural rights, worth protecting. As you progress through this story, you will see why government agencies, with all their resources and good intentions, should not be inserting themselves into families.

Fourteen-year-old Rush, one of the family dogs, waits for the
father to return, but the father could not return – a social worker
said if he returned, his children would be taken away

IT'S A WAR OF TERROR

Donald Wilmot on patrol In Iraq

Feel The Emotional Pain, Consider The Damage

As I begin this chapter, it's been almost four months since the nightmare of government intervention began. There is no sign of it ending any time soon. Tomorrow is August 26th, 2009, my son's twenty-eighth birthday. That's him pictured above, patrolling Haditha, Iraq during the *War On Terror*. His name is Donald Michael Wilmot. I love and care for Donald as much as any father could love and care for his son. Don is my oldest child, a three-tour Marine Corps veteran of the Iraq War. I'm proud of Donald, not because he became a Marine like his father, but because he is *a good man*. Unfortunately for Donald, and myself, and my other

54

great son, Preston, and my wife, Theresa, and my two daughters, Kandice and Davalia, and many other members of our extended family, birthdays like his, and other holiday occasions this year are not the times of celebration and togetherness they should be, or normally would be. Our family won't be getting together to watch parades, blow out candles, attend fireworks displays, cook turkeys, or open presents under the Christmas tree. The reason we won't be getting together is because a *war of terror* is being waged upon us by agencies known as the local police department, the District Attorney's office, and the Massachusetts Department of Children and Families.

Painful Memories Will Linger Forever

As I continue writing, I'm recording the pain and casualties brought on by this terror waged upon my family. Hopefully, the publishing of this book in the future will help other people avoid being caught in a similar situation where they are victimized by the government. Furthermore, maybe this book, when read by people involved in law enforcement, social services, and the court system will cause positive change to occur in the system that allowed this tragedy to happen.

Mother's Day, Memorial Day, my own fiftieth birthday celebration, (they only come once in a life time) which would have been on May 25th 2009, Father's Day, the Fourth of July, Davalia's birthday, Theresa's birthday, Preston's birthday, Don's birthday, and the upcoming Labor Day weekend, will all go down as days of tremendous sadness for our family. But the sadness, the terror, and the sense of loss won't end there. Keep reading on further because you won't believe what happens as the story unfolds. It drags on through Kandice's birthday in October, on through Thanksgiving, Christmas, and New Years, and then forever thereafter as the family breaks apart, kids runaway and become pregnant, and a life is destroyed. It's enough to make a grown man cry – and it has.

CONSIDER THE IMPLICATIONS

A Christmas morning before government intervention

Hopefully, at this early stage of this book, you are starting to gain an appreciation of how life-changing it is when the government intervenes into a family unit with wanton recklessness. Right now, even though no one has died, I am a man in painful mourning. My self-defense mechanism is to engage in intense prayer and thought, while my physical defense mechanism is to workout extra hard at the gym each day. During the process, enlightenment begins to occur. Sad truths become obvious; I see the emotional pain this episode is causing my in-laws, especially Aunt Debbie and Meme, Terry's sister and mother, who are twin pillars of the extended family unit.

Another revelation during the enlightenment is that I'm probably the only person who fully comprehends the reality that none of the state and local agency employees involved in the assault on the Wilmot family actually cares about the lives and reputations they have destroyed since Mother's Day, or will destroy in the future. The thoughts of this huge loss never stop. There is no "putting it this aside" and "just moving on," as some people will eventually suggest that I do.

The anguish has reduced me to a paralyzed man who carries a giant sense of loss and despair everywhere he goes. These feelings have replaced the enthusiasm and joy for life which I had months earlier. The cause of my paralysis is clear cut; public servants have destroyed my family, my life, and my purposeful life, and *they do not care about it in the least*. It's an act of disrespect to a man in monumental proportion. Social Services have never called me personally, or written a detailed letter to me explaining their actions or intent, which in itself is a stark indication that this episode really is a war, and that they have decided that I'm an enemy combatant to be destroyed, and as such, they have no obligation to me.

The whole affair is mind-boggling. <u>A man has but one life to live</u>. It's irreplaceable. You or I can't run down to the store and purchase another life after the one we have has been ruined. The same goes for a family unit. Once an intact family has been shattered to pieces, it can't be reassembled. A new family of the same caliber and uniqueness simply can't be bought. The same is true of my reputation. I can't go buy a new "reputation" to replace the one that has been tarnished by actions of the state. These are some of the things I know more than anyone else at this very moment.

Not Just Emotional, But Spiritual, and Life Altering

The damage caused by public servants is not just physical, but emotional, spiritual, and life-altering. People working for the state not only forced me away from my family, they also ruined a marriage of twenty-eight years, ended my oldest son's new marriage, disrupted and shook the world of my second son, and allowed our two young daughters to run through the course of the toughest years of their life without the guidance and protection of *their good shepherd*. That good shepherd would be me.

The damage caused by the wrongful intervention is financial too. The public servants, perhaps believing they are engaged in a just cause, have robbed me of the ability to earn a decent living, causing an extreme financial setback just when organizations such as the *Wall Street Journal,* and *Good Morning America* were expressing interest in my post-Marine Corps life efforts, but, on account of the pain and sense of loss, and on account of being driven away from my home and office in the garage, I am unable to continue my independent work, be productive, or respond to media inquiries because I am more or less critically wounded.

It's A David Verses Goliath Situation

No matter how hard I try, I still can't fathom how this situation could have happened – we had a great family with so much love and support for each other, then suddenly, out of nowhere, strangers just appeared at the door, broke up the family, and took my life and happiness away. There are heavy, dark pains of disappointment, and huge legal battles hanging overhead as I watch my home from a distance, witnessing the ongoing damage being done by public servants who are operating under a blanket of idiocy and institutional blindness.

The damage is especially severe for the two young girls whom my wife and I *exerted* so much effort in helping. Each day is extremely difficult for me, and I question how I can pull myself through it. There is no one I can turn too, no designated, uncorrupted authority to put a stop to the injustice which is being perpetuated against me, and my family. The state is in complete control. They are so powerful while I'm but one man. It's truly a David versus Goliath situation.

FAMILY BACKGROUND

**An undisputed history of unity, openness,
support, and eating together as a family**

Is This A Family That Would Tolerate Abuse?

Information in this chapter describes the background,
education, and occupational achievements of both parents, plus
family structure and activities up to the point where the family was
destroyed by public agencies. This background information is
included so that readers can form an opinion concerning the
character and abilities of the Wilmot family, and the probability of
either parent abusing their children. Your assessment of the
family's background is useful when considering the implications
of what has been done to the family under the "pretense of helping
them." Once you review this affair, and the qualifications and
strength of the Wilmot family, and the effort they put forth as
parents, you may form an opinion that what has been done to the
family by public servants may indeed be a criminal matter, where
people should go to jail.

The Wilmot family, shown above after attending
Sunday church services, was a tight-knit family, strong
enough to take on the responsibilities of foster parenting

Marine Corps Birthday Ball in Okinawa, Japan (1993)

The Wilmot family consisted of the parents Mark and Theresa. Both had been raised in Central, Massachusetts. Mark met Terry during a blind date arranged by relatives while he was on leave from the service during 1979. The two had a low-cost wedding in Worcester, Massachusetts, then after completing marriage counseling sessions required by the Catholic Church, they were again married, this time by a Catholic priest in the Marine Corps base chapel located at Quantico, Virginia. Both Mark and Theresa came from intact, supportive, and loving families. Mark and Theresa have never been arrested, nor been the subject of any criminal, or legal complaint, not once, not ever.

The Wilmot's first child, named Donald, was born in Virginia during the summer of 1981. Four years later, while living in Worcester, Massachusetts, Mark and Terry had their second son, Preston. Shortly after Preston was born, Mark, who was still serving in the Marines, received orders to report to Marine Corps Air Station Tustin, California. The young couple established a residence in Southern California. They continued living a few miles south of Disneyland and Los Angeles until 1992, when they were transferred by the military to Okinawa, Japan. During these early years of family, Donald and Preston had frequent trips to the playground, plus trips to Disneyland, several oceans and zoos, and every other place a child would love to visit.

Theresa's Education & Occupations

Terry took up an interest in the medical field during the late 1980's, earning her certification as a back office medical assistant. She gained employment at a pediatrician's office, working there full-time, and gaining considerable experience with young children until her employment ended when the family moved to Japan.

When the family arrived on Okinawa, Terry continued her education, but this time it was in conjunction with the Red Cross Dental Assistant Program. Upon graduation, Terry volunteered to serve as an unpaid chair-side assistant to Navy dentists during the next two years. When the family returned to the United States, Terry was experienced and qualified in the dental and medical fields.

Learning Life Skills & Traveling At A Young Age

Donald and Preston attended American schools while living in Japan. They participated in soccer, swimming, and martial arts activities during their spare time.

During the Spring of 1995, the Wilmot family returned to the United States, landing at Los Angeles International Airport in California. They purchased a used Chevy Suburban vehicle, and a twenty-one-foot camping trailer, before driving across the country together en route to Jacksonville, North Carolina. While stationed in North Carolina, the family camped out until they found a house. At that time, Mark served in several command leadership capacities. These included assignments as a Ground Safety Officer, and as a Total Quality Management Facilitator. After his selection to the rank of Master Sergeant, he became the Avionics Division Chief, and Communication Security Chief of a Marine Expeditionary Unit Helicopter Squadron.

Mark & Terry Become Foster Parents

During their stay in Jacksonville, the Wilmot family attended church at Infant of Prague Catholic Church. It was there, in the parking lot after Mass, that another couple suggested they consider becoming qualified foster parents. Because they were spiritual people, who desired to help others whenever possible, they became interested in this new adventure. After being screened by the Onslow County Department of Social Services, and after receiving training from social services, Mark and Terry became certified foster parents. They first took care of a young boy with a history of violence and manipulating women.

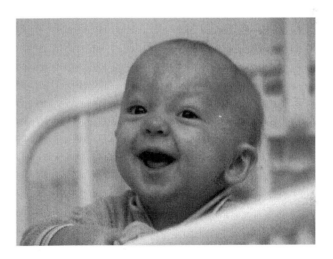

Mark and Terry excelled at bringing joy to babies

To become certified foster parents, Mark and Theresa completed
formal training with North Carolina Social Services

Next, they took on a case of a baby girl who had lost the will to live in a syndrome called *failure to thrive.* Through great love and nurturing, the Wilmot family was able to revive, and ignite the living spirit in that little girl, bringing her back to life.

The Wilmot family unit was strong enough, and trustworthy enough to take on the responsibilities of foster parenting, providing special care for a total of ten foster children

A number of other children came to live at the Wilmot home over the next few years, most notably, Kandice and Davalia, two sisters who had been at another foster home for a short time. The other children who came to live with the Wilmot family were named Leroy, Kim, Michelle, Matthew, Mark, Kerri, Ariel, Hailey, and Tanisha.

The Wilmot family, Mark and Terry, and Preston and Donald, sacrificed their time, energies, and efforts to take care of these foster children. The day eventually came when Kandice and Davalia were adopted by their maternal grandparents. The Wilmots sadly said goodbye to the girls whom they loved with all their hearts.

By some twist of fate, and for undisclosed reasons, the adoption by the grandparents failed. Kandice and Davalia were returned to the Wilmot home in Jacksonville. The Wilmot family welcomed Kandice and Davalia back into the family, then volunteered to adopt them. *After being screened* by the Department of Social Services, the Wilmot family was approved for the adoption of the two girls. This rounded out the Wilmot family for a total of six people, Mark, Terry, Donald, Preston, Kandice, and Davalia.

The Wilmot family, Christmas morning, 1998

BEFORE AGENTS ARRIVE

**Wilmot family members cared deeply about each
other and everyone gave each other hugs on a daily basis**

Normal Family Life

One month before the arrival of social service workers and
police officers at the Wilmot home, the family was intact and
functioning with the exception that Donald, the oldest child, was
stationed in North Carolina. The family did have several challenges
facing them as does every family. Life is dynamic and fluid, and
those with families of their own will understand that personal
challenges always seem to arise when you least expect them. This
held true for the Wilmot family. At the beginning of 2009, Mark
began developing health problems associated with an enlarged
prostate. His physical abilities were further complicated by chronic
asthma. During the same period, Terry was continuing to work
through the pain of physical therapy after having elbow surgery
several months earlier.

Mark Wilmot is pictured above teaching children about fun and fitness during a sports clinic that he hosted.

Terry had been working as a cashier at Walmart, but was out of work while recovering from the elbow surgery.

Mark had been working as an outside salesperson, but for several reasons, including concerns for his health, and plans to launch the new sport worldwide, Mark decided it was time to make an adjustment before it was too late. In addition to planning a summer of fun with his daughters, he established a set of priorities. One of those priorities was to dedicate more time to the launching of the sport he had been working on for more than five years. The second priority was to write several more books. He established goals, then went about accomplishing those goals, working out of the office he had set up in the family's garage years earlier.

Don had joined the Marine Corps during 2004. Because of his test scores, and his impeccable background, he earned a spot in the intelligence field. This meant he went through background checks in order to receive a top-secret security clearance. Between 2004-2009, Donald deployed to the combat zone in Iraq three times.

During each deployment to the war zone, everyone prayed for Don, encouraged him, and sent him greetings and packages. Donald was supported this way because he was treasured by a loving, All-American family. During the Spring of 2009, Don prepared to leave the Marine Corps. He hoped to become a policeman, so he began the application process at police departments around the country.

During March, he made a trip to Massachusetts to take the State Police exam. He scored very high on the test, in fact, he was in the top two percent of seven thousand applicants who took the test. During that trip, Donny had dinner with his family – Mom, Dad, Preston, Kandice, and Davalia. Donald had married Michelle almost two years earlier, after meeting her in Iraq. (Michelle is the person who made the allegations of abuse against Mark and Terry Wilmot). Michelle is described in greater detail in the chapter titled *The Executioner.*

PERCEPTION OR REALITY?

Witch Hunts Did Not End In Salem

The neatly-written statement given to police on Mother's Day effectively portrayed the father of Kandice and Davalia as a complete and total child abuser, and depicted a horrible home-life. Abuse is defined in Massachusetts as the non-accidental commission of acts upon a child under eighteen, which causes or creates a substantial risk of physical or emotional injury, or constitutes a sexual offense under the laws of the Commonwealth, or any sexual contact between a caretaker and a child. Now let's look into this claim;

There was never a sign, symptom, or complaint of abuse. The girls' pediatrician, and school counselors told social service workers there was no evidence of abuse – the girls were fine.

The author of the written statement specifically alleged that Mark Wilmot had mentally, physically, and sexually abused his two daughters since they were about five-years old, a period of almost ten years. It's important to note that there had never been an allegation made in the past, and that zero evidence existed to even remotely suggest that the father had abused anyone, at anytime. Both daughters were happy girls, doing well, especially considering what they had been through during early childhood. *In reality, based on what you learn by reading this book, and other evidence, the *extreme opposite* was true; Mark Wilmot was not an abusive parent, instead, he was an outstanding parent and teacher to all children, and was also a great protector and defender of not just his children, but of neighbors, and of the country. How then can a perception of abuse emerge to overpower the reality of good parenting, especially if educated, professional social workers become involved?

Kandice hugs Davalia during their vacation to Old Orchard Beach in Maine where they enjoyed amusement park rides

Kandice is shown learning how to shoot a rifle at a young age

Loose Brains and Tarot Card Readings

The professionally-crafted two-page statement given to the Oxford police on Mother's day contained twelve *"bullet phrases,"* as if it had been prepared for a corporate sales presentation. As incredible as it seems, the false statement was provided by a fairly-new relative of the family, the daughter-in-law named Michelle Brookfield Wilmot. This is an embarrassing detail, as no one wants to ever have to say that a relative of their own family attempted to do them in. (The root cause for Michelle's bizarre behavior was discovered in the course of research for this book, and is explained in detail in the chapter titled *The Executioner*)

✯Michelle's incredulous collection of clinical phrases, which would normally be seen in a textbook, or in a report written by some type of a mental health professional, concluded with the grossly offensive assertion that both of the Wilmot daughters, ages fifteen and thirteen, feared returning home, and had no desire to see their parents ever again. This sounds very serious, however, is a statement by two injury-free and calm teenage sisters, that they never want to go home again, and that they never want to see their parents again, believable?

Furthermore, has some new legal precedent been established where children have the power to show up at a police station and dismiss their parents?

Is the statement believable considering that both girls ate dinner with their family, hugging their parents good-bye in a routine fashion before leaving the home with Michelle on the Friday evening preceding Mother's Day?

Is the assertion that both girls never wanted to see their parents again believable considering that zero claims of abuse, and zero evidence of any type of abuse existed prior to this statement being given to police?

Should at least one professional on duty have smelled a rat?

You be the judge.

To begin to understand the complexities of what occurred, one must first consider that Michelle might have been suffering from the side-effects of self-hatred, plus several other forms of mental illness, including post-traumatic stress syndrome. This possibility of war-related mental injury, supported by facts, is introduced because a few days prior to the accusation of abuse, Michelle stated that her head had been quite shaken up as a result of being in close proximity to improvised explosive devices (IEDs) blowing up while she served with the army in Iraq. During that brief exchange, which took place in the Wilmot's kitchen, Michelle clearly stated her "brain was shaken, and loose," and that sometimes she "became dizzy" as a result.

No matter what the cause, this woman's judgement was seriously impaired as evidenced by her actions on Mother's Day weekend when she carried out a *preconceived* plan to make allegations against the Wilmot parents, and when she drove past the Wilmot home, instead of stopping to have a family meeting where she could address her concerns of abuse if that was really the case.

Do these children appear uncomfortable with their father, or was there any evidence to suggest they were afraid of him? (No)

One early example of Michelle's abnormal behavior is the fact that she arrived in our home, and quickly directed that furniture and appliances be rearranged in the living room and kitchen. This is a serious breach in protocol. Normal people don't show up as guests at someone's home, then rearrange the host's furniture. I kept quiet over the matter because Terry seemed to be okay with it, however, the fact of the matter is that Michelle was trying to take control of the house and the girls in a subliminal way. Apparently, she perceived me as an obstacle in her way.

★A few days later after the furniture moving, I returned home through the front door, and confronted Michelle as she wandered around the home, waving a canister of burning incense. I asked her what she was doing. She responded that she "was warding off evil spirits."

**The girls were taught by their father the importance of physical
fitness and he often brought them to races where they won medals**

✮✮The greatest indicator she was an impaired person with
ulterior motives is evidenced by the fact that she chose to *drive
past* our home on Mother's Day, on the way to the police station,
where she would construct a great fabrication of abuse. As far as
Kandice and Davalia, they were well-cared for, talented young
ladies with bright futures. Both girls could read music, play the
piano or flute, sing on stage, act in plays, read and write at an
advanced level, draw and paint excellent pictures, cook complete
dinners, plant a garden, explain lessons from the bible, shoot a rifle
and pistol, discuss politics, effortlessly swim the length of the
pool, and run a mile around the track. Despite this well-rounded
developmental success, they were becoming prey to increased
exposure to the heathen culture, and other negative influences,
especially in the public school setting. These influences sidetracked
the girls, pulling them away from the values which their parents
had instilled in them.

**All of the Wilmot children enjoyed a wide-range of recreational
activities in public and there was never an instance of abuse**

They would not be the first teenagers to be negatively affected
by these factors. It happens all the time, so it's up to parents to
maintain control while providing guidance to their children. Terry
and I did this. We set boundaries and restrictions, but not overly
so. Again, aside from the trials and tribulations of the teenage
years, it has to be reemphasized that both of our daughters were
bright and happy, and well-cared for before the interference from
outside sources, including Michelle, and the Commonwealth of
Massachusetts. No signs of abuse existed because the girls were
not abused by their parents.

Both girls were allowed to host birthday parties and
invite their friends, which they enjoyed on many occasions

THE EXECUTIONER

**Michelle Brookfield Wilmot,
character defects unknown**

Who is Michelle? The day before Mother's Day 2009, Michelle was the only daughter-in-law of Mark and Theresa Wilmot. She married their son Donald after meeting him in Iraq during the war. No one could have predicted that the marriage between Donald and Michelle would be destroyed, and legally dissolved before the summer of 2009 ended, and that Michelle Wilmot would go onto to create even more front page havoc at her new place of employment. The marriage between Don and Michelle would be just one of many casualties of the war of terror unleashed upon the Wilmot family by state and local government forces after <u>dubious</u> actions by Michelle.

Michelle completed her service in the army during late 1997 or 1998, then went back to school to acquire an educational credential. To everyone's surprise, she suddenly gained employment in Massachusetts during March of 2009. She traveled to Massachusetts from North Carolina, and began staying over night at the Wilmot's residence in North Oxford. Regrettably, Michelle was allowed to sleep in the small bedroom of Mark and Theresa's two daughters, Kandice, age 15, and Davalia age 13. It was in this small room, that an unstable, confused adult with a self-admitted history of a turbulent childhood, and it's entangling developmental issues, began to form unhealthy and distorted thoughts regarding Kandice and Davalia.

A Struggle With Self-Identity & Image

When Donald and Michelle first met, Michelle was serving in the Army as part of a medical unit. She received basic-level training in the mental health services field prior to deploying to Iraq. As Don and Michelle got to know each other, Michelle presented herself as a strict Catholic woman. When Terry and I heard this, we were excited because we were a Catholic family. Michelle placed the Catholic label over herself in the same manner one uses tin foil to cover leftovers in a dish. The tin foil is shiny on the surface, but is non-revealing, so one cannot actually see or determine what lies beneath. This was the case with Michelle. She cloaked herself under the Catholic veil, while in reality, *based on her actions, words, and beliefs*, was a sort of modern witch, a superstitious mystic, who genuinely believed she possessed supernatural powers.

Michelle was prone to making up stories about her accomplishments because she was eager to gain attention, and win approval of people she met. She was extremely self-righteous. She claimed to be able to speak anywhere from five to seven languages, but that claim may have been exaggerated as it's impossible for the average person to challenge her on these claims. Unaware of her cloaking, and her inner emotional conflicts, the entire Wilmot family became impressed with Michelle as a well-rounded young woman. Everyone accepted her for whom she was with open arms full of family love. Unfortunately for us all,

Michelle was an unknown commodity who had deep-seeded emotional conflicts festering away within the recesses of her soul.

An examination of Michelle's known background reveals she struggled with her own self-identity from an early age, and was in a constant state of inner-conflict. While writing about her service in the Army, Michelle referenced several childhood experiences which contributed to her mental turmoil. Michelle gave Mark Wilmot a copy of her writing the year before. It was the beginning of a book for Michelle, but for Mark Wilmot, it became a window into her soul, and as such Mark Wilmot submitted Michelle's early drafting of her book evidence, item #6, in the trial of Commonwealth of Massachusetts v. Mark Wilmot during July of 2010, and also in the civil rights law suit filed in Federal Court six months later;

"Instead she cried with me, and in our language of tears she told me she knew of my pain. A pain we both knew as children growing up bi-racial, with one side of the family that just didn't accept you. The torment that had lasted through adulthood was happening again. That I wasn't desired for what I was born with, and that once again, something must be 'done' with me. I felt her embrace and in it I felt the absorption of memory. Vivid images of running from a kid with scissors in elementary school yelling "Go back to your country!" Images of when I was left inside a totaled car by my half sister when I was 14. The same sister who tried convincing my Chamorro cousins not to talk to me because I was supposedly this haughty mestiza, a 'half-breed'. People gravitated towards seeing me for just one side or another. A 'half' and not a 'whole'... and I was treated accordingly. Memories of my father's side of the family expressing disappointment that I couldn't turn out with blonde hair and blue eyes like my cousins. Half the dignity, half the respect, half the love, throughout the whole of my lifetime. I built myself up to be a respectable soldier and human being, only to be dishonored again."

✱As a result of her childhood experiences and myths about racism which are perpetuated throughout American society, Michelle developed a self-righteous, defensive attitude, often lashing out at authority figures, especially at white people in positions of power. While recording her story of her experiences in the army, Michelle asked this question:

"Why am I always being persecuted for not being American enough?"

In her thoughts and actions, Michelle may have been reacting partly to her own pent-up anger related to her biological origins, but also to myths she learned about racism and men. Those myths reinforced her distorted mental prism. By viewing Michelle's thoughts in her writings, and comments she made in the Wilmot home, one could easily reach the conclusion she wished she looked different, that she believed she was always being judged by the color of her skin, and that all men were bad, and could not be trusted, all of which are common threads of belief in the blanket of liberal ideology which is constantly thrown over young people on college campuses by people who are pushing their agenda instead of teaching facts and knowledge. It is my belief that most people are not racist, especially most white people, and that most people do not view others by their skin color, but rather by the content of their character as Martin Luther King would have wanted us to.

Michelle's ethnic heritage created a unique personal appearance. That appearance was the result of her mother's Pacific Islander genes, derived from a historically insignificant and little-known tribe of people called Chamorros, and her father's genes, derived from a non-distinguished cross-section of Europeans. As a result of her genes, Michelle could pass as a person from any number of countries or ethnic groups. This fact of life, one's personal appearance based on genealogy, could be viewed as an advantage or disadvantage, depending on one's attitude and upbringing. In my opinion, and based on constant comments Michelle made to family and friends, and in her own writings, she almost secretly harbored a negative interpretation of her self-image, often wishing she could look more like a typical American, if there is such a thing. (There really isn't a such thing as a typical-looking American because we are a highly-diverse nation because of a mixed gene pool)

A Human Chamaeleon

Basic training in the army provided Michelle with a small degree of poise. As she matured further, she developed into the type of woman who could hold her own in almost any situation, and unfortunately, according to her own bragging, the type of woman who could fool people, changing like a chamaeleon whenever it was advantageous to do so. This worked to her benefit on Mother's Day, when she posed as a competent, caring relative of two young girls who "needed protection from their own parents."

One quandary, which is related to the concept of self-image, confronted Michelle everywhere she went; the typical American, male or female, sophisticated or not, could not accurately guess where Michelle was from, or what her nationality was. Some people mistakenly assumed her to be "an immigrant" because she looked different, and because of an erroneous assumption by unenlightened people who still assume all Americans share similar physical characteristics. This unfortunate fact of life, that some people could not figure out where she was from, bothered Michelle a great deal. In other words, she resented the way people initially viewed, and perceived her. In my opinion, this is one of several reasons she developed a dislike of her self-image. Michelle could appear attractive, but she interpreted people's reaction to her uniqueness as racism, which it wasn't, but she chose to carry a self-inflicted wound around with her.

In her story about her troubles in the army, Michelle wrote; *"all my life I was made to taste the bitterness of racial hatred."*

In reality, it was Michelle who could not accept the fact that all people are different, and that some people are just innocently ignorant. Michelle's fellow countrymen were not the only people who could not figure out what nationality she was.

While serving in the Army overseas, soldiers and foreigners alike, were equally challenged to correctly guess Michelle's ethnic origins. This irritated Michelle even more, so she had difficulty operating within the confines of her job while getting along with others. She couldn't accept the fact that things are not always done by the book in the combat zone, and that other people had priorities. In her own words, she demonstrated self-loathing;

"I wasn't a person after all. I was simply this exotic thing for people to observe and investigate, an alien in any environment I was in. Never mind my character, personality, or interests, the first questions from most people in my unit was regarding my ethnicity. Who was I, and where was I really from, as I couldn't really be an American."

In my opinion, Michelle despised her reality, creating her own self-hatred. This became a contributing factor to why she received a disciplinary punishment while serving in the army, why she would later get fired from her new position in Massachusetts, and why she felt a need to strike at the bogey man she created in her head. It's her own words which reveal her seething tendency to act as a judge, jury, and *Executioner, especially* when her anger becomes so strongly internalized that it must burst outward. In the next quote, Michelle describes a meeting with a superior officer who was making a personal effort to bring Michelle "back into the fold" after Michelle completed a forty-five-day confinement type of punishment. In this written passage, Michelle demonstrates her intensity and potential to lash out with vengeance at the person she selects as a target, just as she did in the allegation against Mark Wilmot:

"Dressed in shorts and a t-shirt, she carefully adjusted herself to comfort in her desert recliner under her makeshift parasol as I was out under the blazing sun in full uniform. But that has always been the case hasn't it? Her yoga classes and luxurious romps painfully contrasted against my team scrounging in the desert for supplies like dehydrated beasts. It made me want nothing else at the time but to own a guillotine to make this story come to a justified happy ending."

☆☆☆During 2009, at the same moment her highly-questionable actions destroyed the family she had married into, Michelle began working as the program director at the Northeast Veterans Training & Rehabilitation Center, located in Gardner, Massachusetts. Less than a year into this new position, during April of 2010, problems and conflict again erupted, with Michelle at the center of the controversy. In my opinion, based on my careful analysis, Michelle, the self-righteous, angry woman, had to create a new problem and a new crisis where she could gain attention and get the spotlight upon herself. She spoke to the media at length, and elevated unfounded complaints about how things were being run at the private, nonprofit organization where she worked. In the story, Michelle described her unhappiness which was based on the fact that as the program manager, she was expected to find a way, and the means, to make the nonprofit facility live-up to its initial expectations.

Again acting as the judge, jury, and Executioner, Michelle undertook actions that ended-up on the front page of the local newspaper, not once, but twice. These two newspaper stories would become evidence item #34, in the trial of the Commonwealth of Massachusetts verses Mark Wilmot during July of 2010. In my opinion, Michelle's venomous actions harmed the reputation of her employer. Worse yet, her actions also ended up tarnishing the nonprofit effort to help disabled veterans. Michelle left her position under the cloud of controversy either by termination, or on her own as a result of her behavior and actions. This latest conflict in her life might not surprise all who know her; a review of her young life indicates a pattern of self-inflicted conflict, complaining, and unhappiness with the ways things are, all of which provide clues that something is affecting her state of well-being.

MISTAKEN IDENTITY CREATES EXTREME PREJUDICE

Negligence Allows Faulty Perceptions To Grow

Soon after unwittingly accepting the false allegation by Michelle Wilmot, the Oxford Police and the social services officers made a significant mistake during their substandard investigation. One of the officers requested a CORY check, or background records check as an elementary step in the investigative process to find out whom they were dealing with. Based on what you have read so far, you have a pretty good idea who Mark Wilmot from Oxford is. He is the man honorably retired by the United States Marine Corps during June of 2008 as a Master Sergeant. He is a man who served at the President's Helicopter Squadron, and the designated Communications Security Chief for a Marine Expeditionary Unit, both positions of trust which require a person with an impeccable background. You also learned that

Mark A. Wilmot from Oxford had an outstanding reputation as a great father, not only to his own children, but to ten foster children.

The significant, and inexcusable mistake committed at the Oxford police station was committed by the sergeant on duty, or the investigating officer, or another officer getting involved in what should never have become a case. No matter who made the mistake, a lack of professional competence and attention to details created another toxic batch of character poison which would be added to the proverbial well that Michelle Wilmot had already poisoned with her neat and complete false accusation against Mark Wilmot. What was the significant mistake? The Oxford Police failed to obtain the correct person's identity when they conducted the criminal background check. Worse yet, police and social service workers failed to notice the mistake once it was made. The background check they received belonged to another person named Mark Wilmot, who lives in Arlington, Massachusetts, not North Oxford. This man's father's name is John, his mother's name is Jeanette, his date of birth is during 1957, and he was born in Georgia.

Will The Real Mark Wilmot Please Stand Up

Unfortunately for Mark Wilmot of North Oxford, whose father's name is Donald, whose mother's name is Eleanor, and whose date of birth is during 1959, and who was born in Worcester, the Mark Wilmot living in Arlington had tangled with the law. Seconds after the print key was pressed, the computer terminal communicated with the main frame data base, then replied back to the Oxford printer. Out came a one-page arrest record containing a list of charges including failing to obey a police officer, assault and battery on a police officer, and resisting arrest. As you might guess, police do not look kindly on people who tangle with them.

Gross Negligence

✮✮✮✮✮Even though the printout they accepted at the Oxford police station contained a clearly-printed, capitalized, bold-faced warning in the top section of the page, stating the report was not supported by a fingerprint match, and asking the requestor to verify the social security number and date of birth of the person requested, Oxford police and Massachusetts social service workers failed the simple, yet absolutely necessary responsibility of verifying the identity of the person requested. Instead, public servants investigating a case based on false allegations, accepted a background check containing felony criminal charges against another man with another date and place of birth.

Not only did the public servants involved review this derogatory record – they allowed it to color their judgement while inserting it into the active case file causing everyone to develop a warped sense of reality which led to bias against an honorable man who up the day before had a clean record.

This act of gross negligence remained unnoticed during the development of the case against Mark Wilmot. In the rush to hang a man, the erroneous background record was copied, forwarded, reviewed, and read by countless other people involved in the process. In fact, the record check was printed out a second time, meaning the same mistake was made twice. Eventually, the record of another man became page two of official court document #0964CR2304, used to arraign Mark Wilmot on two charges of assault and battery, and one count of indecent assault at the Dudley District Courthouse on July 2, 2009. That date was fifty-two days after the allegations of abuse were first made. In those fifty-two days, the Oxford police made no effort to interview Mark Wilmot. If they had, they could have perhaps discovered the folly of their preconceived notions and mistakes, and *they could have prevented a family from being destroyed*. However, that did not happen.

A PERSON IS INNOCENT UNTIL PROVEN GUILTY

The Oxford police and social service workers neglected the fundamental, but critically important law of the land which has stood for over one hundred years. That <u>accepted law</u> clearly states that all men are presumed to be innocent until found guilty in a court of law. So, instead of treating Master Sergeant Mark A. Wilmot as an innocent man, and serving and protecting him by affording him equal protection under the law, police officers instead acted negligently, maybe even maliciously, and in the process, may have even engaged in a criminal act (the violation of one's civil rights).

★★★★ At this stage, assuming they had the authority to use any means necessary to investigate an allegation of child abuse, and assemble evidence which would help gain a quick conviction, police officers, including the chief, and the social service workers entered into an *illegal conspiratorial effort* for the express purpose of *depriving* a decent and honorable man and father of his *constitutional rights.* This behavior, contrary to protections guaranteed under the Bill of Rights, and the concept of equal protection under the law, left an innocent man in legal jeopardy and life-altering peril as public servants laid the ground work to have him arrested.

Fair Judgement Is Impaired By Prejudice & Bias

There was already a great deal of prejudice generated against Mark Wilmot of Oxford because of the effectiveness of the great fabrication and the three-party plot hatched on Mother's Day. This creation of perception became coupled to the institutional group-think, and preconceived notions of the people connected to the arena of child abuse. When the newly-formed awareness of a person with a prior record of assault and battery on a police officer, and resisting arrest was overlaid onto this pre-existing condition of prejudice, one outcome was almost certain to emerge – all people involved would develop extreme prejudice and bias against Mark Wilmot of North Oxford. The only way to prevent this growing prejudice and bias from affecting one's judgement and decision making abilities would be for each person involved in the arena of child abuse and law enforcement to be <u>truly concerned</u> about families, and truly concerned with following procedures and regulations without abusing power, and most important, <u>honoring the constitutional rights of everyone as a matter of habit</u>.

✯Again, it must be stated, that up to May 10, 2009, Mark Wilmot of North Oxford was a man who had never been previously charged with a crime. He had never been associated with a criminal proceeding, except to come to the aid of law enforcement officers on several occasions during his lifetime, one occasion in which he received a heroism award for his actions. With the above information in mind, is the 14th Amendment of the Constitution applicable?

That Amendment says;

"...No State shall make or enforce any law which shall abridge the privilege or immunities of citizens of the United States; nor shall any state deprive any person of life, liberty, or property without due process of law; nor deny to any person within its jurisdiction the equal protection of the laws."

A group of newly-freed men gain protection from the Fourteenth Amendment, which now protects all Americans

The 14th Amendment was ratified in 1868, shortly after the Civil War. It was created to ensure that the rights of former slaves (freed by the 13th Amendment in 1865) would be protected throughout the nation. The need for the amendment was great, **to guarantee equal protection for everyone**, because up to this time the provisions of the Bill of Rights were not enforceable against state governments. This was due to the case of *Barron v. Baltimore* (1835). In this case, the Supreme Court held that the provisions of the Bill of Rights were enforceable against only the federal government (and not against state governments). Without an amendment justifying federal intervention in the affairs of the states, states, (especially local law enforcement agencies) who were still hostile to the interests of the freed slaves might still legally discriminate against, or persecute them. So the new amendment made it clear; everyone, under every circumstance, is deserving of equal protection.

A TEAM APPROACH TO
DESTROYING A MAN

**Picture after picture, plus eyewitness accounts illustrate the
exceptional relationship Mark Wilmot had with his daughters**

Three days into the investigation, after the proverbial well had
been poisoned by the total effectiveness of Michelle's voluntary
statement, and after the acceptance of the criminal record check on
the wrong Mark Wilmot, a cross-agency team of investigators
gathered at the Leicester Police Station. The purpose of this
meeting was to interview Kandice and Davalia while a hidden
camera recorded the event. The people on the investigating team
stood behind a large panel of one-way glass observing the
interview. They have already developed a perception which is not
based on reality. Rosie Alicia, the forensic interviewer is the wife
of the Wilmot's local state representative, a fact which is just as
pertinent as the fact that the local police chief is the brother of the

school superintendent, and people working for the court have relatives throughout the legal system. On account of serving the country and being away from the geographical area, Mark and Theresa Wilmot are not connected to any informal network of relatives and lifelong friends, so no close review of the facts takes place, and no benefit of the doubt is extended. The *hunt* is on.

Kandice and Davalia, carefully nurtured by both parents in a loving and safe environment, wave during a summertime party at their home. During the SAIN interview, government agents coldly labeled Kandice as Victim #1, and Davalia as Victim #2

One week earlier, Kandice and Davalia were two innocent girls from a nice American family, traveling through adolescence, and more or less enjoying life as teenagers. Now the state is involved in their life. The state assigns new names to the girls during this process of intervention. Kandice becomes Victim #1, and Davalia becomes Victim #2.

Victim #1 is first to go into the interview room. Theresa Wilmot, the girl's dedicated, loving mother, is not allowed to observe, or participate in the process. She is given the cold shoulder treatment by the public servants, and is told to wait outside in the hallway with Victim #2.

I'm not invited. I've been told I can't return home, or my daughters will be taken away. I fear for my personal safety on account of the way the situation has been unfolding. I am developing a distrust of the process on account of the way the public servants have conducted themselves, especially when it comes to following their own procedures and accepted law. They are using soviet-style tactics on my family, but it is happening right here in Massachusetts, under the guise of "helping children and families."

✭✭✭The public servants are clearly violating the rights of the family during this proceeding. The details of the taped interview remain undisclosed, but it's important to note three discoveries made during my investigation into what transpired up to this point. Those discoveries contaminate the accuracy of the interview in favor of the people who are already biased and prejudiced against an innocent man. Before describing those discoveries, I would like to mention at this point in this book that I studied basic and advanced criminal investigations at Central Texas College, receiving an "A" in both courses, so I'm confident the following discoveries, and my overall conclusions in this book are accurate and factual;

(1) Michelle set Kandice and Davalia up, creating a scenario of total abuse because she was emotionally unstable, had unresolved anger issues, and had impaired judgement.

(2) On the way to the police station on Mother's Day, Michelle coached the girls on how to answer questions, saying she had been through this type of process before, and instructed the girls to review written study notes so their stories would match when questioned separately.

(3) Once the children were done at the police station on Mother's Day, they drove home with Michelle. On the way home,

and while parked outside their home, both girls reviewed a copy of Michelle's professionally-crafted statement, giving them a chance to learn and memorize Michelle's extensive descriptive vocabulary.

Total Parental Involvement

As a father, Mark stayed totally involved with his children. In this picture, he is shown with Davalia and Kandice as they prepare to stay overnight at a girl scout camp in Spencer, Massachusetts

Kandice and Davalia, being raised as young ladies, the family motto being "smart, strong, and a good person"

★★★★★These activities and conditions, the studying of written notes on the way to the police station, the coaching by Michelle, and finally, the re-reading of Michelle's written fabricated statement, <u>caused the girls to internalize the claims of abuse</u> constructed on paper, i.e., most of what Kandice and Davalia said from the time they arrived at the police station, to the responses during the recorded SAIN interviews three days later, can be directly attributed to the formation of a storyline, and the *parroting of events* which Michelle constructed through the extraction and conversion of innocent revelations.

The young girls came to believe they were abused while the professionals surrounding them were encouraging them to believe it too, as if it was the goal of the process. The "created facts," or story line, became etched into their minds, i.e., both girls internalized the re-creation of innocent acts, and the fabrications through a process associated with the laws of learning, i.e., the laws of intensity, recency, and repetition. The entire interview process, with police, social workers, and prosecutors, is contaminated – the results are illegitimate. Despite this reality, none of the "professionals" involved are aware of this enormous procedural flaw. Why is that? Do they have any concern for the Wilmot family?

Kandice sits happily at the dining room table making Christmas cards at age 15. A year later, with her father gone, and family structure and unity broken by social services, Kandice enjoyed more freedom with less supervision which contributed to her becoming a pregnant, unwed teenage mother of two children

THE GREAT FABRICATION

An Interesting Effort To Make The Charges Stick

In her handwritten statement to the Oxford Police, Michelle succeeds in creating a wild fabrication which instantly destroys the reputation and credibility of my wife and I. Based on her past experiences at fooling people, Michelle believed she was clever enough to get away with it.

In order to establish a cover story for the big deception, Michelle innocently claims that on May 9, 2009, Kandice and Davalia, suddenly and without specific cause, began disclosing a lifetime of physical, sexual, and emotional abuse at the hands of their adopted parents. Michelle creates the distinct impression this revelation of abuse was an unexpected, spontaneous event. This is not the truth.

It's Best Described As A Foxy Scheme

A review of what actually occurred during the days leading up to Mother's Day shows that Michelle orchestrated the affair by employing a clever strategy to accomplish her emotional need to *execute* someone.

Her foxy scheme begins with suggestive reasoning and coercion techniques to introduce the topic of abuse to Kandice and Davalia. This fact is certain as there was never any prior claim, discussion, suggestion, sign, or evidence of abuse in the family before Michelle arrived at the Wilmot residence during April. In the course of her actions, Michelle will claim that ten years of abuse took place, and she will do it without any evidence to support the allegation. In my opinion, she does this because she is blinded by pent-up anger and bitterness, and because she has developed a dislike of omnipotent white men. Her premeditated campaign to elect Mark Wilmot as an abuser required that she set the girls up to begin believing they were abused. The second stage included the isolation of the girls from their family during Mother's Day weekend. During this stage, I believe that Michelle began fantasizing that Kandice and Davalia could end up in her care, living with her in a home she planned to purchase in the coming weeks. It's a strange motive to consider, however, Michelle's inner mind is in a state of extreme conflict, so the generation of this thought leaves the fantasy stage to become a clear objective. While looking at a home to purchase, Michelle told the girls in her company they could live with her, even saying that a high school and college were nearby, and suggesting they could attend those schools.

Understanding How A Person Thinks Is Relevant

★★★★★ Make note of this important causal factor as you read this version of events; Michelle was in the United States Army, and served for a short period in a live combat zone. She does not think like a civilian. *She thinks in military terms.* Believing she could be a good spy, she seeks employment with government agencies such as the CIA and the state department.

Michelle actively goes after this line of work because she has a history of successfully cajoling and fooling different types of people when she came of age, and she views her skill sets as being a match for high-level cloak and dagger operations. Agencies must have passed on the opportunity to hire Michelle, because she never got hired there.

⋆Once the pre-project planning of Michelle's latest mission was accomplished, and she had the girls to herself, away from their home, she finished laying the foundation for the allegation. Through friendly and innocent conversation, Michelle proceeded to extract as many singular events as possible, being careful to probe into any area which might yield productive intelligence.

⋆Kandice and Davalia, a bit angry at their restrictive parents, are no-match for the cloak-and-dagger motives behind Michelle's back and forth probing. They think it's neat to have a cool sister-in-law who loves giving them advice, videos, and music downloads. Michelle has even taught them how to belly-dance to exotic, Third-world music. These are all things that their parents could not provide, but Michelle could. Michelle is an outlet for the girls. They feel free from the constraints of their parents. In a short time, she becomes a trusted confidant. She probes deeper whenever she senses an opportunity to gain advantage.

Military People Are Often Mission-Oriented

Michelle is mission-oriented at this point. She is an army of one. She selects certain events which can be twisted, then converted into something they are not. Michelle's intent and actions are sinister throughout the whole affair. Examples of Michelle's conversion of innocent events, into a dishonorable event, include the misrepresentation of the daily hug given by Mark to his children. This normal activity by a caring, nurturing parent, is converted by Michele into daily episodes of inappropriate contact which "made the girls feel weird."

A second example of an innocent activity being twisted into something more sinister is the tradition of the father making an annual trip to the mall with his daughters during the weekend after

Easter. The purpose of this annual trip was so the girls could pick out new bathing suits for the coming summer. This annual shopping trip was sickly twisted into an instance of inappropriate activity with the girls through Michelle's manipulation. Using this technique, Michelle reworked and reshaped many of the father's actions, suggesting to the girls that the father had dishonorable intent.

The Process of Manipulation Requires Skill

✶During this process of manipulation, Michelle succeeded in working the two young girls into a confused frenzy. In this confusion, they were mere putty in Michelle's hands. Because they were mad at their father, and because they considered him a major obstacle to unconstrained freedom with boyfriends, telephones, and peer activities, they were almost eager to go along with Michelle's contrivance that their father was a bad man. The final act of this horror show was for Michelle to execute the man she had chosen as a vessel in which to vent her pent-up anger.

✶Starting at the top of her statement, Michelle strayed away from reality, claiming that sudden revelations of abuse took place at her current place of residence in Ashburnham, Massachusetts. This was not true. Michelle had not yet established a residence in Massachusetts, a fact which will be introduced in court. Although she slept over at her new employer's home on several occasions, the majority of Michelle's nights from March until May were spent sleeping in Kandice and Davalia's bedroom. These are important details, because they reveal Michelle's thought process as she begins constructing her great fabrication.

In addition to guiding and protecting his children, Mark made it a habit to give his children a hug and kiss at least once every single day, all the way up to May 8th, 2009, always telling his children how special they were, and how much they were loved. There was never a complaint about this daily hug until Michelle extracted information about the girl's lives, reorganized it, then persuaded the girls that acts of parental affection and nurturing by their father were inappropriate and dishonorable.

Kandice hugging her father as he sits on the couch

A Premeditated Plan

Another notable discrepancy in Michelle' statement is that during an outing with Theresa Wilmot one-week earlier, Michelle began probing the subject of sexual abuse. During one specific conversation with Theresa on May 2, 2009, Michelle directly asked Terry if the girls had ever mentioned being abused by their maternal Grandfather who had since died. Surprised by the line of questioning, Terry provided a negative response because there had never been any evidence, nor a complaint of any inappropriate activity. This conversation, one week earlier, factually demonstrates that Michelle had developed preconceived notions which matched her predisposition and distorted thought-process on the subject of abuse. This predisposition led Michelle to create a situation where manipulation of facts could take place.

There is other proof that Michelle is lying about conditions surrounding the revelation of abuse. Further down in her statement, she writes that the mother is "aware of abuse" but now denies any knowledge of the abuse. Michelle never spoke with Theresa again after Kandice and Davalia supposedly revealed they had been abused. Michelle references her husband Donald in this section, getting confused as to how to cover the tracks of her inconsistency. In other words, Michelle forgets she never spoke with Theresa again after taking the girls away on a weekend trip, but in her report, she references a conversation about abuse that took place before there was a revelation of abuse. In her fabrication, Michelle portrays two young girls who say they do not want to return home, but is it believable?

Prior to their departure on the May 8th trip with Michelle, the Wilmot family had supper together at the table. Everyone enjoyed a normal conversation, with one exception; Michelle made unusual, eyebrow raising comments seeming to justify physical abuse on children, such as, "if I acted out as a child my face would be rubbed in the dirt."

Again, it's important to consider that Michelle thinks in a military-style, covert manner. So, in retrospect, it appears as if Michelle was "laying cover" before putting her plan of action into motion with the created allegation of abuse against her husband's father.

HOW THE PHILOSOPHY OF ABUSE AFFECTS US

Words The Girls Do Not Use

In the opening paragraphs of the allegation, Michelle contends that Kandice and Davalia state their father instigates verbal and physical confrontations with them. This is the fourth notable objection to the truthfulness of Michelle's statement. This objection pertains to the use of vocabulary in this paragraph, and throughout the statement as the vocabulary is not consistent with Kandice and Davalia's word portfolio at their age and stage of intellectual development. For example, the girls would not use the word "instigate" but Michelle applies it to her statement. In another one of the sentences, Michelle states both girls claimed their father engaged in "inappropriate touching," "leering," and "the making of sexually inappropriate comments," (all words and phrases which are not found in either daughter's vocabulary).

☆If Kandice and Davalia are not the original source of these words and phrases, then where did they come from? The truth is that Michelle got several ideas for her accusatory vocabulary from the federal government's work place sexual harassment poster!

My rebuttal to the wild accusations is that aside from diaper changing and health-related actions when the girls were young, there had been <u>zero</u> instances of me placing my hands into the outer clothing, or into the inner clothing, or the outside of the girl's sexual anatomy, and that aside from parental conversations at the dinner table, or in the living room area, concerning warnings of unacceptable behavior, there have been <u>zero instances</u> of sexually inappropriate comments made to the girls. Furthermore, it is quite a leap of speculation that a father would be "leering" at his children, or that his children would tell someone, "My father leers at me." This illustrates how Michelle is manufacturing allegations of abuse against the father.

Distortion ed Prevents Rational Thought

⋆During the early stages of the affair, Michelle commented to the girls that "she sensed something was wrong with them," going so far as to suggest she could feel such things because she had "supernatural powers." At this stage in the analysis, it starts to become possible to comprehend Michelle's motives and actions. Michelle arrived at erroneous conclusions about child abuse because she was interpreting information filtered through her own distorted mental prism. In my opinion, the thoughts and judgements she formed concerning Kandice and Davalia became tainted by her own childhood experiences, her military experiences, her unstable emotions, and her anger. But there were more contributory factors to her makeup.

The New Philosophy Seeps Into The Culture

Another contributing factor in this affair, and this again is based on my opinion after reviewing the facts I could get my hands on, and based on a theme I heard repeated in college classrooms and other campus settings, and then repeated again by Michelle in her casual conversations, is the fact that her adult mind-set was partially shaped by the new modern language and philosophy of abuse which has evolved over the past thirty years. New college courses, and even degree programs, and child abuse initiatives, and domestic violence awareness seminars are in vogue now. The politicians are more than happy to get into the act by speaking on the subject, or passing new laws because it makes them look good. And again, there is television, helping to build-up, then perpetuate the politically correct hysteria that child abuse and domestic violence are huge problems in American society. Last but not least there are sufficient numbers of angry women who are re-channeling their shortcoming and negative experiences into this orientation which is subliminally undermining men's rights and manhood. For some people older than forty-years of age, the topics of child abuse and domestic violence remain controversial as far as their full legitimacy as bonafide problems in American society, but who can argue against being over-reactive without

107

being made into a villain? The condition we are in now occurred because some, but not all of the claims and statistics used to raise the level of importance of abuse and domestic violence is based on conjecture, falsehoods, and agenda, so much so that it has now become common for more and more young people to claim they have been abused, while fewer older Americans are willing to support such a claim.

In the years after their adoption, the father ensured the girls learned all essential skills while at the same time providing them with many opportunities to get exercise and have fun

Over the years, the girls enjoyed time spent with Dad

Michelle Wants Payback

During conversations with Wilmot family members, Michelle alluded to abuse by male relative(s) at a young age, while also claiming to have been heavily-pursued by men who made unwelcome advances toward her into her adult years. On top of that, she also alleged that her biological father was abusive toward her mother. So, in my opinion, Michelle became a proactive prosecutor in her own right. She planned to get "payback" for all the perceived wrongs done to her and her mother, and she viewed herself as feminist freedom fighter. But there was more to it. She was overly-fond of the girls. She fantasized about making them her own. This is why she had a distinct course of action in her mind. Michelle's vision would quickly convict the man, and free the girls up so that they would live with Michelle, as if they were two dolls. Yes, it sounds crazy, but the truth is that Michelle wanted the allegations to be true because she desperately needed to unload her own personal torture which had been bottled-up inside for so many years.

Remember this, Michelle's claims are being made despite the fact that both Kandice and Davalia have never reported any type of abuse, and have never been seen for abuse or injury, and have never complained of a single incident of abuse.

If Mark Wilmot had abused the girls in such a manner as described in the statement, there would have been physical injury because of the contours of the inner walls of the Wilmot house, and if such abuse occurred, Preston Wilmot, the twenty-four-year-old son living at the home, or Mrs. Wilmot would have intervened for safety's sake, and for the righteousness of the cause because everyone knew right from wrong. No one in the home would ever have hurt the girls.

The Evidence Suggests Father Was A Good Parent

The most important rebuttal comment of this portion of Michelle's statement comes from reviewing the typed letter that Mark once wrote to Davalia *in response* to her request to attend a school dance. This letter was recovered by the police from Davalia's boyfriend's house. It was reviewed by social services and police investigators. Even though it proves contrary to the false allegations, it was included in the court document as if to support the claim. The letter was in direct response to a letter from Davalia to her father. That letter from Davalia has since been recovered, and will be included as evidence in court.

In his response to his daughter's request, Mark Wilmot writes back, "I have observed your growth and development, and effort this year," a comment about Davalia's progress as a child growing up. The father then writes such comments as "Conditions of going to the school dance include dressing and acting like a young lady," plus the statements that, "Davalia put maximum effort into school work, and "that she read and study more each evening," and "that she consider changing her hair style so her hair is not in her face."

The father ends his thoughtful response to his daughter's request with the words, "Keep up the great work, you are a treasure to me, today, and always and forever."

This illustrates how Michelle takes real events from the girls' recollections, and twists them and reformulates them in order to construct seemingly lewd transgressions by the father against his daughters. Michelle's trickery is exposed because the original letter written to Davalia, and other like it still exist. Michelle did not anticipate this possibility.

Another entry by Michelle alleges "physical abuse against both girls within the past week," but Michelle lists no details or specifics of this claimed event. Mark Wilmot's rebuttal to this is because there were not any incidents during the past week. The next entry states that "the father was directly demanding them not to go to the police or school counselors."

Since no incidents or complaints of abuse were made by the children, no such demands or comments could have been made to the girls. There has never been a discussion of a need to go to the police or counselors, (except advice to maintain privacy on their adoption and family situation) so this comment again demonstrates a bias by Michelle to build a damaging image of the Wilmot home which is based on exaggerations or misinterpretations of comments by the girls.

THE USE OF CLINICAL TERMS

In the written allegation made on Mother's Day, Michelle's use of language is professionally clinical, but it goes unnoticed by police and social service employees. The reason is because her vocabulary matches perfectly with the cognitive template of people in social services. It's the type of phraseology used professionally, phrases that Michelle has perhaps seen before, and the truth is, she has. Using a military analogy again, Michelle writes (fires) for maximum effect, using words and phrases as if they are bombs. She drops them in the right places, to completely destroy the intended target. Michelle closes her statement with a wild claim that "both girls fear being placed back into the system" as foster children, and that both girls fear returning to the house, and most outrageous of all, that they do not wish to have "any communication or interaction with their parents."

Kandice and Davalia have no recollection of being in "the social service system," so how could they have a fear of going back into it? This is proof that Michelle fantasizes that authorities will award her custody of the girls because she is "their savior."

Questions arise how police officers and social services investigators missed this huge warning flag which clearly points to a hidden motive behind the allegation. Furthermore, how could officials have accepted the fantastic claims at face value considering there was no evidence to back it up?

Davalia learned how to play the flute and the piano

☆☆In response to these sentences by Michelle, it is again so very clear that she is the driving force behind the complaint, and as crazy as it seems, wants the girls for her own, as if they were dolls, or items of possession easily moved from one place to another. Michelle had made unusual, envious comments about Kandice and Davalia's hair and skin color in the past. This is another point of reference related to her difficulty in accepting whom she was, and how she appeared to others. The truth is that if Michelle was not a sick person, and did not have ulterior motives, she would have returned to the Wilmot home after hearing of an allegation, and either requested, or demanded a family meeting.

Kandice is shown receiving piano lessons

Again, the evidence is clear – there were no prior complaints of abuse by the girls, and no signs of trauma or unhappiness, however, both girls recently had arguments with their parents over excessive cell phone and internet usage, and both girls were trying to gain more freedom away from the house in order to have unsupervised time with their boyfriends, both of whom had been pressuring Kandice and Davalia in what might be considered the typical ways of a teenage boy.

Michelle writes in her report that both girls are "terrified," and have a history of suicidal ideation and gestures which were unreported by the mother. The rebuttal is that Michelle is tapping into her medical vocabulary and experience in mental health to construct outright false statements which support her goal. The truth is that both girls were going through adolescence, and that's it. Michelle ends her statement with the claim that "Kandice and Davalia have no desire to have further contact with their parents." Now ask yourself this question; *Do children now have the option of abandoning their parents on a whim?*

The warning flags missed by police and social services; Michelle had an unusual fondness for Kandice and Davalia, and strongly desired that Kandice and Davalia live with her, suggesting this at least three times during the allegations once to police, once to social services, and suggesting it within her fabricated statement.

Are there any competent adults on duty anymore, or has complete idiocy taken over? How could police officers and social service workers have missed this great big red warning flag which demanded that officials proceed with extreme caution?

Michelle's biases, her memories of her father, and the complaints that her mother made about him, plus all her unhappy experiences, and her distrust of men, led her to betray and destroy her new family through this complaint in which she had fantasies of becoming the girls' caretaker. At this point in her life, Michelle is a mentally unbalanced person, who has committed several crimes in the process of her contrivance.

✶The sad truth is that Michelle was maliciously effective during her slick *presentation*. She had already prepared the young girls for the interview by having them study cards on the way to the station so their stories would match. The great fabrication made on

Mother's Day was accepted without question or doubt by investigating officers, followed by the social service investigators, the case workers, and persons at the District Attorney's office. Then it became an official part of the court document.

Finally, as public servants, whose defined mission is to serve and protect, the Oxford Police Department should have noticed the unusual nature of this sudden complaint. They should have been curious if foul play was at work. They should have proceeded with extreme caution, with concern for the reputation of a man, with professionalism, perhaps interviewing the reporting party further to discover hidden motive before notifying anyone, or taking unjustified action which could cause permanent damage to the reputation of one of the town's citizens while destroying a functioning family unit along the way, i.e., public servants should have been concerned with two legal considerations; equal protection under the law, and the legal consideration which states that all men are innocent until proven guilty.

Kandice and Davalia had a close and loving relationship with their mother and Aunt Debbie, their mother's older sister. Debbie's husband, because of his community service with the Exchange Club, possessed expert knowledge on the subject of child abuse, so Debbie and Steve, who had frequent contact with both girls, would have easily detected any signs of abuse, and would have intervened on behalf of the girls, as anyone in the family would have. Police and social service workers never attempted to interview Debbie or Steve, or any other relative of the girls during the investigative process.

GROSS POLICE NEGLIGENCE

**Oxford Police, and social service investigators never bothered
interviewing Mark or Preston, who lived in the home, or Donald,
the husband of Michelle, or other relatives, or neighbors**

Why Leadership & Training Is Important

★★★According to the Constitution and subsequent
amendments, all citizens are guaranteed *equal protection under the
law*, and further, no state law may undermine, or subtract from
every single person's constitutional rights. Applied to the situation
described in this affair, it means that parents and children must be
afforded the same rights and treatment of equal protection under
the law. Said another way, one type of person, no matter what their
age, and no matter what agents of the state claim, can receive more
protection under the law, or greater rights than another person.
Adhering to this principle of law helps guarantee fairness and
justice.

To even a casual observer, it would seem that the unusual
nature of the voluntary statement made to police on Mother's Day,
and the seriousness of its contents, would have grabbed the

attention of a professional in law enforcement. A person with some degree of training in law enforcement would surely have become curious, perhaps even intrigued by the complete damning nature of voluntary statement being made in the absence of concrete evidence to substantiate the claims.

A trained and alert professional would scrutinize the information, and the person standing before them to some how validate the statement's truthfulness *before* jumping to conclusions.

It would also seem that even a typical police officer, in a typical police department, would sincerely desire to screen out, or validate a fantastic claim of abuse against a man because of the officer's *genuine concern for the reputation* of every local citizen, and especially *the constitutional rights* of every local man, and the rights of every parent in town. We would all hope that we have an adequate level of protection against the potential of a witch hunt which could be based on a false allegation.

Most people will admit that men are at a distinct disadvantage in situations where there is an accusation of any type against a female. That's the way it has become in American society. That is why public servants need to follow the law. The considerations described above, and a small degree of concern for a good man's rights never materialized on Mother's Day in Oxford, Massachusetts. No such professional was on duty at the police department to methodically separate perception from reality, and fabrication from fact. No such person was available to call a time out in the game of life, and determine if there had been a flagrant foul. Instead, police officers who had sworn to uphold the law, accepted a malicious fabrication, then triggered the unleashing of powerful forces of the state. These well-funded, unchecked forces were unleashed upon an unsuspecting American family.

In my opinion, the person on duty to greet and interview the three girls on Mother's Day might have been lazy, incompetent, untrained, or a combination of all three. Or maybe that person watched too many television shows such as CSI, and Law & Order, where entire cases get wrapped up in less than one hour of television. Or maybe the gross negligence took place because the town's police chief failed to establish a policy of notification, and checks and balances on unusual events, or maybe the officer did not follow procedures. No matter what happened, no one showed evidence of a concern for the parent's rights to equal protection under the law, or what might happen if the police got it wrong, and went down the wrong path.

The Execution Of Dirty Tricks – Passing The Buck

When this affair first started on Mother's Day, my wife and I did not realize the police department was already operating in a criminal investigative manner. If this was true, then it would seem that an officer would have to have been present to give the Miranda Warning to everyone in the family. My wife and I had heard back from a lawyer who recommended that we inform social services that we would be seeking legal representation, a right that Americans possess in all legal matters. We requested a meeting the next day, which would be a Monday, with social services to discuss the allegations with an attorney present, but employees at the state agency never responded to this request, or to my phone calls on the following days. Why not?

What was happening behind the scenes is that another dirty trick was being executed – the proverbial slipping of a card under the table, done under the pretense of following the law, and "protecting children." This dirty trick used by social services is called the making of a *referral* to the District Attorney's office. In this case, records show APM Susan Connelly made the referral to the District Attorney. This was all accomplished on the basis of a wild allegation, without supporting evidence, or the completion of a real investigation.

This severe course of action, done without a cautious and fair inquiry, is how social services passes the buck, and pretends they are not involved in the criminal prosecution of a family member for a crime against another family member. Maybe that is why they never had to appear in court even one time against Mark Wilmot, even though they destroyed his family and his life on the basis of a wild allegation.

What does it all mean?

What it means is that when a family somehow becomes entangled with social services, its members actually come under an attack from three entities – the Department of Children and Families, the Police Department, and the office of the District Attorney. The implication of this is that people involved in making decisions which affect people's life, are not accountable for their actions.

✯Remember, the Constitution and the Bill of Rights guarantees all citizens equal protection under the law, and the amendments have been upheld in court stating that no state law may undermine, or subtract from every person's constitutional rights. There is even a law on the books that provides for a small penalty for persons who violate another's constitutional rights;

Chapter 265: Section 37. Violations of Constitutional rights; No person, whether or not acting under color of law, shall by force or threat of force, willfully injure, intimidate or interfere with, or attempt to injure, intimidate or interfere with, or oppress or threaten any other person in the free exercise or enjoyment of any right or privilege secured to him by the constitution or laws of the commonwealth or by the constitution or laws of the United States. Any person convicted of violating this provision shall be fined not more than one thousand dollars or imprisoned not more than one year or both; and if bodily injury results, shall be punished by a fine of not more than ten thousand dollars or by imprisonment for not more than ten years, or both.

PUBLIC SERVANTS FAIL TO PERFORM THEIR DUTIES

Fifty-two days after Mother's Day, I stood in the small district court building located in Dudley, Massachusetts, deprived of my constitutional rights, my family broken apart, my life falling to pieces. The disturbing fact here is that I had never been interviewed by the police, or the Department of Children and Families even though they claim they completed an investigation into the allegations of abuse. Police and the social services investigators also failed to interview Preston and Donald. Both of these good men, sons of Mark and Terry, big brothers to Kandice and Davalia, would have been able to provide definitive information which could have refuted the false allegations of abuse that Michelle claimed took place over a ten-year period.

★★★As curious as it seems, the police did manage to find time to visit Davalia's boyfriend's home, where intimidation came into play. According to Gage, the police ordered him to search for a letter that I had written to Davalia several months earlier. Gage saw that letter, and asked Davalia if he could keep it because he liked the photograph that I had inserted above the text. This letter actually helps prove the allegations of abuse made against me are false. According to Gage, he felt intimidated by the police when they insisted that he go for a ride to the police station to answer additional questions. Afraid of what they might do to him, Gage complied with the authorities.

★Once they were at the station, Sergeant Green or Sergeant Hassett suggested, persuaded, or demanded that Gage provide a written statement. This statement would be used to bolster the case against Mark Wilmot. Not understanding the implications and legality of the officer's actions, and thinking he was doing Davalia a favor, Gage complied with the officer's request. This action occurred before Davalia recanted her story of abuse. So, without any firsthand knowledge of any occurrences in the Wilmot home,

Gage gave the police what they wanted by fabricating a distasteful and extremely damaging statement which further poisoned the well of evidence. (Gage has since expressed regret over his actions.)

✯✯✯Armed with this new information, a false statement by Gage, the police brought Davalia back to the police station to question her for a third time.

Remember this critical point; they brought Davalia back to the station to verify what someone else had written in a statement. Davalia read the statement written by her boyfriend, then spoke to the police without reservation, saying the contents of Gage's letter were not factual, and did not occur. That did not matter. The witch hunt for evidence against Mark Wilmot demanded results. So, instead of being professional, and conducting a legitimate investigation by visiting the boyfriend a second time to clarify and verify what he had said and written, Sergeant Green included the false statement in the court document because it supported the built-up criminal charges he intended to file against Mark Wilmot.

✯✯✯✯ This effort to induce or pressure a young boy to produce a statement, followed up with a failure to validate a hearsay statement illustrates yet another instance of the selective investigation of facts and circumstances. This lapse in professionalism can be directly attributed to the environment of extreme prejudice and bias which was first created by Michelle's fabricated allegation, and secondly, by the criminal background check which was based on the mistaken identity of Mark Wilmot. Now everything was being compounded by poor performance and a lack of professionalism by officers involved.

Liabilities Of An Under-Qualified Police Chief

One of the most incredible indicators of gross negligence, and unprofessional law enforcement behavior occurred when I called the Oxford police chief during June, about thirty days into this affair. Before I relate what happened, please read the quote below. It is taken directly from the official Oxford Police Department web site. In the quote, Chief Michael J. Boss, the brother of the local school superintendent, was being paid in excess of eighty-thousand tax-payer dollars each year as the chief, explained his law enforcement philosophy;

"We spend as much time talking about customer service as we do about crime solving. I have always felt that we in government service are not always going to be able to solve your problems, make you whole, or make you happy. The one thing we can do is always make sure you know that your problems are important to us, and that we will do anything we can under the law to help you."

Now that you have read the chief's open letter to the public, consider how he treated a good man from the community when that man called the station for much-needed help. The purpose of my phone call to the chief was to inquire what was going on because my wife and I were still uninformed of the whole matter – completely in the dark. Social services had ordered everyone not to discuss the matter, meaning we could not talk it over with our own children!

Once I made contact with the chief, and explained who I was, and why I was calling, the chief refused to discuss the situation with me, saying, "I can't discuss this with you because there are some serious allegations against you."

I attempted a second and third time to explain that there must be a mistake so we could communicate, however the chief refused to discuss it further as he terminated the conversation.

As a witness to the facts recorded in this book, what do you make of the chief's performance? Do you feel he is qualified to be in a leadership position, or do you feel the town fell into the trap of hiring him because his brother was the well-liked superintendent of the Oxford Public Schools? Is the town liable for the professional negligence of the chief and his men who contributed to the destruction of a good family, and the loss of my reputation and liberty?

The reason I mention failed performance and gross negligence is because the chief has left the town open to a civil rights law suit.

He failed to act, and failed to ensure his officers had the proper training to serve and protect.

The chief claims in his web site letter that officers *"must complete 40 hours yearly of in-service training which consists of CPR, First Responder, Law updates, and Firearms Qualification. We also have Officers specifically trained in such areas as Child & Elder Safety, SWAT Training, Accident Reconstruction, Criminal Investigations, Drug Investigations, School Resource, and Cyber Crimes."*

What important subject is missing from this in-service training, and what critical element of law is not mentioned anywhere on the police department's web site? The answer is the *United States Constitution.* The lack of awareness of constitutional rights and equal protection under the law, and a general lack of leadership within the department contributed to the injustice of this story. Consider the applicability of the sixth amendment;

*In all criminal prosecutions, the accused shall enjoy **the right to a speedy trial,** by an impartial jury of the state and district wherein the crime shall have been committed; which district shall have been previously ascertained by law, and **to be informed of the nature and cause of the accusation; to be confronted with the witnesses against him;** to have compulsory process for obtaining witnesses in his favor, to have the assistance of counsel for his defense.*

It's already been mentioned but it's worth repeating; the investigating officer(s), Officer Hassett and/or Sergeant Green, who made a special trip to Davalia's boyfriend's house, and obtained a statement from a fifteen-year-old, made no attempt to interview me during the so-called investigation. Nor did the police officers involved with this case make any attempt to interview our son Preston, who lived in the home where the alleged abuse took place.

Marine Corps Sergeant Donald Wilmot, briefly returned home to Oxford during March of 2009, and scored a 100 on the Massachusetts State Police exam. The family looked forward to him returning permanently during the summer, however that homecoming would never happen on account of negligent and wrongful actions committed by police and social services.

Sergeant Green did speak briefly to my son Donald by phone, primarily because Donald took the initiative to call Sergeant Green several times. Donald was married to Michelle but had returned to his Marine Corps unit in North Carolina after scoring a one-hundred on the Massachusetts State Police exam. Donald suggested to Sergeant Green that police interview Preston. This suggestion occurred after Green admitted that he did not know there was another son living in the Wilmot home. Does the absence of a fair and cautious effort by local law enforcement sound legitimate, fair, or professional?

Does the performance of this public servant seem like something you are willing to put up with as a citizen?

In my opinion, the Chief of Police and some of his officers, failed miserably, both in their duty, and their obligation to the townspeople in a most profound way. Keep in mind that I'm speaking as a Master Sergeant of Marines. Maybe I'm just a little too competent because of my past experience as a leader, but if I was away from the base for the weekend while serving on active duty, and a significant event occurred – anything out of the ordinary, including one of the Marines in my unit being found drunk on the side of the road, or a police report of domestic violence by a service member, or the arrival of a national security message, then I would expect a phone call from the marine on duty at the base.

At a minimum, I would discuss the situation and provide guidance to the person on duty. That advice would include boundaries on how best to proceed. At a maximum, I would get up, put on my uniform, and proceed to the base to carry out my responsibilities of command and leadership.

One thing is for certain; the person standing duty over the weekend shifts would not be making phone calls outside the command, or calling up the commanding general without going through me first. This is the correct way of doing business, not just in the military, but in any structured municipal department, or business. If a serious incident occurs in any town on the weekend, or on a holiday, then the chief should be notified right away, in fact, if this common sense procedure is not established in a policy letter and discussed during training, then serious administrative flaws exist within that department.

So, the Oxford police chief should have been personally involved in this case on Mother's Day, before any phone call was made to the friendly folks on duty at the Department of Social Services. If that simple procedure had been established and followed – an officer on duty checking in with his boss about a sensitive situation with the potential to become a television story on Sixty Minutes, and if the chief was a properly qualified man, possessing the wisdom and good judgement that comes with maturity and experience, then great damage to people's lives, and the destruction of the Wilmot family unit would never have occurred. For me, the performance of the investigating officers, the supervisors, and chief of police is an issue to follow-up on with the Board of Selectmen in the town of Oxford, and in a civil-suit action, at which time I will be asking for restitution for damage done to the Wilmot family, and my reputation and life. Once that is accomplished, other parties who contributed to this case of injustice will also have to be held accountable. For the reader, this aspect concerns you in the sense that you would want your local governing officials to be wary of selecting the wrong person for a leadership role, especially if the selection process is based on any factors or information other than qualifications, sustained performance, good judgement, and overall professionalism.

A picture of Kandice and Nick, attending their first high school formal (before government intervention)

JUST ANOTHER CASE

**Can a man protect his liberty, get justice, and keep his
freedom without good performance of the court system?**

Does Anyone Really Care?

The order generated by the local court, directing that I remain
away from my oldest daughter, was a binding order created by the
quick movement of a pen, held in the hands of a government
lawyer working for the local District Attorney's office. This man
knew very little of what he was doing on July 2nd, fifty-days after
a relative fabricated false allegations, touching off an emergency
response by the state. The public servant automatically checked off
a small box on a court document without being overly-concerned
about the far-reaching ramifications of his administrative powers.
He was just acting out his part in a very bad system consisting of
feel-good laws, public agencies, court systems, and the people
working within those systems. I was not questioned by the judge
during this five-minute court hearing, nor was I was offered an
opportunity to speak. Not a single police official involved in filing
the charges, or a single person from the Department of Children

and Families appeared at the hearing. Why? The judge did not question the veracity of the information which created the proceeding that he was now presiding over. Why? Not one person in the court room was on guard to question the circumstances surrounding this unexpected arraignment which started when an unstable woman conspired with two teenagers to utter a malicious statement containing the worse kinds of falsehoods, which police failed to properly investigate. My wife and I did not know it then, but we would end up attending eleven more court hearings during the next year as our wonderful family was destroyed. Worse yet, at each of those trial dates, no competent authority would question the validity of the whole proceeding, while various public servants, who were responsible for perpetuating the gross injustice, working for the Department of Children and Families, and the Oxford Police Department, failed to show up in court a single time.

The only thought I could think about was that in the future, a law suit would have to demonstrate that due-diligence, and even a small degree of the fail-safe protection of a citizen's constitutional rights did not take place on Mother's Day, 2009, and that gross negligence occurred during the months that followed. The perfect storm had happened, and Mark Wilmot was caught in the middle of it without a life-preserver.

A Father Is Arraigned In Court
So, I stood there in the court room on July 2nd 2009, in shock, but not shame. The reason I was in shock is simple. This could not be happening to me. When I look in the mirror, I see myself not as a criminal, or person guilty of a crime, or as an abuser, but as a great citizen, an excellent father, a caring family man, a good neighbor, and a real American who will stand up for constitutional rights. While I stood there in court, and in many moments since, it seemed like I was a nobody – not a man, not a citizen, not an American. By the brisk manner in which the arraignment was proceeding, I was not worth an ounce of respect – not three minutes of real time in the courtroom, which could have been spent extending some degree of courtesy, and the benefit of the

doubt to a man who surely deserved some respect. After all, there was no evidence that abuse took place. All that existed was an *allegation,* written and presented by a mentally-impaired person. In the time period since Mother's Day, it could have easily been proven this person possessed a psychological defect which aroused her to create a false allegation with premeditation and vengeance. No one listened to my wife or I, or read my statement of innocence which suggested that officials investigate the person making the allegation. Instead, professionals overreacted, responding with a witch-hunt mentality which allowed perceptions to overtake reality.

Does A Man Deserve The Benefit of Doubt?

I think I deserved a little respect. I think I deserved the benefit of doubt. Now my life has been stolen. I think I deserved the right to keep my family intact, to have my children and wife in my arms. Now my happiness is gone. I think I deserved the right to run my own family, and the right to solve our daily problems without interference of people with other *belief systems* and goals. Now my liberty has been taken. Looking back on it, I think I deserved *my constitutional right to life, liberty, and the pursuit of happiness.* Instead, I became just "another case" in an unjust system where professional scrutiny and good judgement seemed to be lacking.

Kandice and Davalia, shown above before government intervention, and before a court order was issued, ordering Mark Wilmot to stay away from his daughter Kandice. This order, issued without any judicial review of the circumstances of the case, remained in effect for over one year. It was vacated after Mark was found not guilty of assault. During this period, the Department of Children and Families became the surrogate parent, replacing Mark Wilmot as head of the household, an action with life-altering, negative consequences.

PERFORMANCE REVIEW OF SOCIAL SERVICES

Whitinsville, MA – The windows of the social service building are masked by one-way blinds, and the front entrance area contains a receptionist stationed behind bullet proof glass, which contributes to the atmosphere of agency secrecy and unquestionable authority

A Recent Court Ruling Against Social Services

The Founding Fathers never envisioned, and took steps to prevent the federal government from growing as large as it is today. They would never have thought it prudent that the federal budget would include the funding of payments via a national system which encourages the state-sanctioned abduction of children from good homes, so that those children may be placed in other people's homes, and followed-up on by government workers whose job security would be threatened if there were no "cases" in the system which employs them.

As awful as this sounds, it really happens. In one instance during December of 2008, a Massachusetts social services agent wrote a letter to a judge, asking that the department be allowed to

133

take a baby away from a mother who had previously lost custody of two other children. There was one big problem in this case; the baby had not been born yet, and the mother had done nothing which could justify her losing her newborn baby.

Despite these facts, a judge in Massachusetts leaned a little too much in favor toward social services. Instead of leaning toward constitutional rights of an American, the judge automatically ruled in favor of the Department of Social Services. What happened next? In a pre-planned, state-sanctioned abduction, social services agents swooped into the hospital right after the baby was born, and took the baby away from the parent.

Attorney Dorothy Meyer Storrow of Greenfield, Massachusetts got involved in the case, taking the matter up with state's highest court. Eleven months after the state- sanctioned abduction, while I was writing this book about my own experiences with social services, the Supreme Judicial Court of Massachusetts ruled that the judge who made the previous decision, and the Department of Children and Families moved too fast in taking the child away. The court further ruled that the constitutional rights of the parents, and a right to due process cannot be over ridden at the whim of government workers. This may be good news for the Wilmot family when it comes time for a court proceeding to address civil damages to the Wilmot family. The next section explains why this case is headed toward more than one courtroom.

A Conspiracy Against A Family

As shocked as we were, Terry and I believed the situation which erupted on May 10th, 2009 would be over as soon as reasonable people grasped the details behind what caused the commotion to begin with. After all, there was a simple explanation why there might have been a complaint against us as parents. There certainly was not anything that justified the need for social services to be involved with the family in any manner.

⋆Terry and I did not even begin to understand the manner in which the Department of Children and Families, i.e., Corinne Contarino, Susan Connelly, Justine Tonelli, Mike Polenski, Kevin

Foley, Jeff Fogle, Ken Carlo, Tara Tracy, and others, and the Police Department, i.e., Chief Boss, Officer Picard, Officer Hassett, and Sergeant Green, could *as organizational agents of the state, conspire* to deprive us of our constitutional rights, and how they would work against our best interests as Americans, and the best interests of the family. We repeatedly requested to have a meeting with the Department of Children and Families, starting as early as May 11th, so we could discuss the situation, and put an end to the matter. They took messages, passed the buck, and told us to call them the next day. However, our phone calls to the agency went unanswered. The method these public servants use to avoid dealing with parents whose family has been attacked and who want answers, is by call-screening, answering machines, and/or explaining they have to check with their supervisor on a particular situation. This lets them off the hook. In reality, many social service workers pretend to be too busy to return people's phone calls. This makes them un-accountable to anyone who is not in their chain of command. The fact of the matter is that they are all accountable to you and I the taxpayers.

⭐The day after Mother's Day, the police department and social services, joined forces with the District Attorney's office in secret cooperation which can only be viewed as an *arrogant conspiracy* to entrap Mark and Terry Wilmot. Terry thought she was safe, and Mark was the target, but anything could have happened at this early stage. Terry could have been charged with a crime too. That is the reactionary mode the public servants operate in – helping families is just a smokescreen for them to accomplish their intent. During the one year following the attack on his family, the head of the household father never received a single letter of correspondence from social services, meaning there was a distinct effort to deprive him of information and an opportunity for legal recourse.

Social Services Ignores Calls From The Parents
While we are waiting to resolve the matter as quickly as possible, Terry is directed to bring the girls to a "forensic," tape-recorded interview at the Leicester police station. This interview is

scheduled three days after the Mother's Day attack on the Wilmot family. Never having had interaction with the authorities before, Terry and I remain ignorant of the looming reality that we are in great legal jeopardy, and that our family and life will soon be destroyed. We are not aware of this reality because it simply could not happen in America to a good family like ours, or could it?

Days and weeks passed without a response to our inquiries even though the social workers were visiting the public schools and inquiring about the children. School officials described the Wilmot girls as normal students who seemed to be doing well.

Again, it's critically important to again note that during this stage, Terry, Preston, Kandice, and Davalia were blindly following the unlawful order made by authorities which forbade them from discussing the event among themselves. I've been the head of my household for the past twenty-eight years, but now I'm living under the threat of having the children I love and care for taken away.

✶Essentially, I am not allowed to return home. I've been told that I can't have contact with Kandice and Davalia, so I'm not able to bring resolution to the crisis as I normally would do as the natural leader of the family.

On June 16th, Sergeant Green was still actively seeking a copy of text messages sent from Terry's phone on the day before Mother's Day. Records show that Sergeant Green has already decided to charge me with crimes, but most curiously, he had never requested to speak with me. Lacking common sense, but committed to nailing me to the wall, Officer Green was under the erroneous *assumption* that evidence of abuse could be derived by obtaining the text messages. He has already decided to file charges against the father, so he is really searching for evidence to support a foregone conclusion based on his own judgement which is based on faulty information, bias, and prejudice.

Total Professional Malpractice

On June 23rd, social service worker Tara Tracy, and supervisors Burns and Gemski met at their Whitinsville office to discuss the Wilmot case. Ironically, this discussion was held in the absence of Mark and Terry Wilmot. During this meeting, Tara Tracy recommends keeping the case "open" because as she puts it, "there continues to be a question about the level of risk the children may be exposed to with their father".

✭Before you find out what Tara Tracy recommended to the team of social workers responsible for the government's on-going actions, pause for a moment to consider what has transpired up to this date, which is an incredible forty-three days after the false allegations were made; Mark and Terry still do not understand what is going on. They both deny the allegations and can prove the allegations are not true. Government agencies are using their considerable resources and expertise to attack and weaken the Wilmot family. The allegations put forth on Mother's Day, and the direction of the case continue to be intentionally hidden from the family. Why hide things from a family? Terry and I talked about it. Terry did not blindly accept my denial of abuse, but asked me point blank if I had ever done anything that could have caused this allegation. My answer is no. Terry knows I'm telling her the truth.

✭We review every possible incident in our daughters' lives which could somehow have been misconstrued. We come up empty-handed, because there is nothing which could constitute abuse. In our minds, we know there is nothing anyone can say about how we raised our children. In our hearts, we know our children have not been abused.

✭Although there is no concrete evidence of abuse, and even though pediatricians and school officials state the girls are fine, Sergeant Green continues to look for anything to support his foregone conclusion that Mark Wilmot is a sinister villain who must be put away in the slammer for as long as possible.

✭Up to this point, Tara Tracy and Sergeant Green have never attempted to interview Mark, Preston, or Donald Wilmot. Preston lives in the home. Donald also lived in the home during the majority of the ten-year period when abuse of the two girls allegedly took place. Both Preston and Donald would have been the first to *volunteer coherent information* to validate or refute the wild allegations that were made by Michelle.

It's blatantly obvious that the social workers and the police were not even slightly interested in finding out who I am as a father, and my version of events. They don't know much about my personal history, my experiences, my convictions and beliefs, and my qualifications as a parent. Much of the information they have developed is inaccurate and distorted. They are committed to pre-judging me to get the conviction. The image they have created in their minds and in documents is based on bias, the false allegation made to the police, and the erroneous police records check.

A Truly Outrageous Recommendation

So now it's June 23rd, over six weeks since her department swung into emergency action. Tara Tracy sits at a special department meeting, with at least two other educated, trained social service professionals. At this point in time, Tara Tracy is very much aware that school officials have reported the girls had been doing fine up until Mother's Day, with no signs of anything being wrong. She is also aware, through what Terry has repeated, that the girls were adopted, and that they did have a difficult start in life, and furthermore, that other factors, including teenage rebellion, contributed to their recent actions in relation to Michelle's allegations. Tara Tracy knows that on Mother's Day, both Terry and I denied the existence of abuse. She knows that the two investigators ruled out sexual abuse on Mother's Day, and that Kandice has stated that her father never hit her. She also knows that on Monday, May 11th, that I provided a typed letter of disagreement to social service investigator Mike Polenski, his supervisor Ken Carlo, and the forensic interviewer, Rosie Alicia. That letter clearly stated that I was innocent of any wrongdoing. In the letter, I also informed the department that there was no basis for an investigation, and that zero incidents of physical or sexual abuse had ever taken place.

✶Armed with all this information, Tara Tracy addresses her coworkers as if she was a competent professional. She advocates that the case be elevated another few notches on the scale of criminality. Although there is no evidence of abuse, and both parents deny abuse, Ms. Tracy presents a recommendation that two young and innocent girls begin treatment for sexual abuse. The outrageousness of this social worker's gross incompetence does not stop there. As the meeting continues, the arrogant and over-assuming social worker proceeds to go way beyond the boundaries of reason and judgement by further recommending that I be screened as a sexual offender. It's at this stage that a man with an outstanding reputation as a father and as a citizen is being maligned without justification. This truly despicable recommendation is grounds for civil damages and termination of the social worker for malpractice. Think about it!

Despite the fact that a legitimate investigation had not been conducted, and a meeting and discussion of the Wilmot family affairs have not taken place between the parents and the social service workers, people at this public agency are on the verge of making judgements and decisions with huge implications! (The sex offender label is the modern day scarlet letter) The questionable recommendations are approved at the meeting that day, then put into writing in a document called a service plan.

✶Just like the court document which was generated by Officer Green or Hassett, with the erroneous police records check, the service plan written by Tara Tracy is reproduced, printed, and distributed a countless number of times, meaning reputation of Mark Wilmot is tarnished even more, while people reading the service plan become that much more biased.

The service plan recommended I undergo sexual offender evaluation, and that the girls undergo treatment for sexual abuse. It was determined there was no sex abuse on Mother's Day, yet this insidious recommendation had made its way onto a government document that will be reproduced countless times. If this type of outrageous action is happening on a regular basis to innocent people, it must be stopped by a public outcry. Think about the damage this can do to family members and their reputations.

To illustrate the harmful implications of this action by government workers, consider if social services recommended that a person undergo a psychiatric evaluation in place of sexual offender screening. A recommendation to be screened for mental illness is to suggest a person is crazy. So, a recommendation that a person be screened as a sex offender is tantamount to suggesting they have committed sex crimes. Using this same logic, by suggesting that the Wilmot daughters undergo treatment for sexual abuse is to imply they have been sexually abused. The fact of the matter is that there never was any abuse of the girls, and there certainly never was a claim that sexual contact, or any amount of sexual activity occurred between the father and his daughters. This creates more questions;

What are these public servants thinking, and what is their competency level? Are the public servants who claim to care about children and families so acclimated to a belief in the validity of their subject matter, and so intent on making everyone a victim and a perpetrator, that they become judge-mentally crippled by group-think, which is then solidified by a complete lack of common sense? Is this atmosphere fertile for negligence and malpractice? Is the system broken and out of control?

SO, WHAT DID HAPPEN TO THE MAN NEXT DOOR?

**The Department of Children & Families, and local police,
using false information and conspiracy, broke up a family,
then replaced an excellent father with a group of social workers**

The Gaping Hole In My Chest

It's Thanksgiving Day as I write this chapter. Six months have passed since the war of terror began. You already know I'm no longer living in my home, I'm in exile. Donald and Michelle are already divorced. Worse yet, Donald is not coming back to Massachusetts as planned. My dreams of being a patriarch of a strong nuclear family have slipped away, stolen by agents of the state. The collateral damage caused by the government's actions continues to add up. Although she is still standing by me while I defend myself, my wife Terry, who has been under extreme pressure, has befriended another man for support, and has decided our marriage is over after we get through this event. I'm devastated. If I was not such a strong person, and if I did not have people providing love and support, I'd have already checked out because my life and happiness have been stolen. The anger caused by the government's intrusion into our family does not lessen but there is no outlet for it except to write this book. There is something really, really, wrong with what has happened. I lie awake each night, remembering events big and small, and thinking about every detail and conversation. In my mind, I examine each new fact as it surfaces, always looking for the answer as to how a perfectly good family and life could possibly be destroyed in the manner in which it has. There is constant pain in my heart. It's hard to explain, but it feels as if there is a gaping hole in my heart. I wish I could pull it off, and toss it aside as if it were a foreign object. The source of the pain is both the trauma of the initial event, and what has transpired every day since. As a father, and as a man, I have been separated from my home, wife, children, dogs, work, and personal belongings. I live out of my truck and sleep on an air mattress while I am prevented from continuing on as the leader and core support of my family. What I don't know at this point is that the trauma, the pain, and the injustice will continue for many more months, and that one year from now, after staying with close friends, I will have become factually homeless as I attempt to start a new life in southern Florida.

There is no one to turn too. No competent authority, just a system with too many people who lack common sense and an appreciation for constitutional rights. My lawyer has told me I can't prove that I'm innocent. He says I have to wait it out, and let them try to prove that I'm guilty. I don't agree with this state of affairs, but I cannot return home. If I do return there, and come in contact with my daughter, agents of the state, backed up by members of the local police force (militia), will forcefully take our daughters away.

If I return home, the local police will arrest me while almost certainly using undue physical force. They think I'm a felon with a record, a real trouble maker, because of the false allegation and the erroneous background check. So, going home, or even driving around the town of Oxford puts my life in further danger. The situation feels like something that would happen in the former Soviet Union, or maybe down in Mexico, where citizens are routinely assumed to be guilty by a corrupt justice system. But I'm not living in the former Soviet Union, or in Mexico. I'm a citizen of the United States of America, and this story is happening to me in Oxford, Massachusetts.

Terry and Kandice at the park in Auburn during 2007

THE FAMILY DISINTEGRATES

Michelle and the Wilmot children pose in front of the Oxford Town Hall, after Donald returns from his 3rd tour in Iraq

A Growing Family With A Bright Future

Prior to the Mother's Day attack by government agents, the Wilmot family of North Oxford consisted of two married couples, the parents Mark & Terry, their son Donald and his wife Michelle, and Preston, Kandice, and Davalia, all with a bright future. As a result of the forced social service intervention, both marriages were over. Donald finished his tour of duty with the Marines. Instead of returning home to Massachusetts to be a policeman as he originally intended to do, he decided to stay down in North Carolina. Preston, feeling a great sense of disappointment over the destruction of his family, moved to a shabby apartment located in the nearby city of Worcester.

Rush, the oldest family dog, was put to sleep because there simply wasn't anyone to take care of him as he required extra attention in his older years. After living out of his truck, and staying with relatives and friends, and wary of chance encounters with local police, Mark ended up moving down to Florida, trying to heal from the devastation. This left Terry, Kandice, and Davalia living alone in the North Oxford townhouse which was once a vibrant home, filled with loving support, guidance, encouragement and family dinners where members spoke freely, and listened and loved each other. By November of 2010, only Theresa and Davalia remained in the home. Is this a desired outcome? Are the girls in this story better off now, without the rock-solid family they once had, and without the daily influence and guidance of their father? Have the girls been harmed by the intervention and government actions? How many thousands of tax dollars have been wasted, and what will the future cost be?

During Mark's absence, Terry survived with emotional support from friends and several neighbors such as Greg, a man living next door to the family (Picture taken during neighborhood cookout)

Kandice was affected by early childhood circumstances and teenage turbulence. She required strong parental supervision which she was receiving before the state intervened.

The answers are easy to arrive at. By December of 2009, Kandice had become emotionally entrenched in a lonely void where she truly believed she was a victim of abuse because people had coached her, and pigeon-holed her into this state of mind. Having people believe her, and winning a case against her father became important, as was more time to be with Nick, and her other friends. With Michelle still lurking in the background as her potential ally, Kandice felt her back was up against a wall, with no avenue of escape. Her relationship with her mother depreciated. The rebellious attitude of a sixteen-year old took over. On a cold December night, with the wind-chill around ten degrees, Kandice packed up some clothing bags, wrote an insulting note to her mother, saying she was running away to live with one of her friends. Coincidentally, the friend she chose to run to was the one who had introduced her to the dark and evil side of life, which is what pulled Kandice away from values of the Christian philosophy, and pushed her toward the Wiccan religion and the allure of unnatural and unhealthy acts. If I was home, in my rightful place as head of the household, this would not be happening. Now all I could do on this night was to pray for Kandice, the miracle I had given so much love too, the miracle who was now putting herself into greater jeopardy on account of the government's war of terror on the Wilmot family.

Kandice survived that cold December night, and returned home the next day. However, her life was still the life of a child traveling through adolescence, and she needed her father more than anything.

The Trap Of Victimhood

By February, Kandice's relationship with Nick came to an unexpected end. Depressed and undermanned at the parental staffing level, Kandice spiraled further downward into the trap that victim-hood presents. Her therapist recommended a trip to the emergency room for an evaluation. That trip to the hospital occurred, followed by an extended overnight stay at another facility, and the introduction of prescription medicine. All this time, her father, the head of the household, the leader of the family, the one who had been her good shepherd, watching over her, teaching her, guiding her, is out of her life. He is prevented from helping her because he has been unjustly sanctioned by the state, then replaced with a team of social workers who probably care more about their vacation days and pension plans than they care about the safety, stability, and future of the girls that the Wilmot family placed so much effort and love into bringing up as their own.

Pregnant With Two Babies

The incredibly sad truth this affair became worse during May of 2010. That is when Davalia ran away from home. So, in the course of a year, both girls had been ordered into therapy at the direction of social services, placed into lock-down facilities, given prescription drugs, and subsequently both girls had become teenage runaways, and then to top it off, Kandice became pregnant with twins at the age of 16, and left home at the age of seventeen to live here and there.

During the time of intervention, in the absence of her father, Kandice wrote the following letter to her boyfriend. The letter demonstrates how Kandice says and believes things that are not based in reality or fact, but more so in theatrics;

Dear Nicky,

Some things are left silent in my mind. Unable to surface, for if they do, I fear I'll be scarred again. You can see me unlike anyone else. I'm scared and insecure, but I'm strong. I have a will to live now, when before it would be better to die

In the process of finding myself I got sick. I'm an addict to painkillers. (A complete fabrication or element of imagination) I've been off them for a while. But I get tired, weak, headaches, muscle aches, and depression. I'm not going on meds or painkillers, I'm fighting the effects. I know I let you down before but I'm doing this for myself and for you.

I have mental trauma and am just catching up to my age. My mom and dad did drugs, before, during, and after my birth (referring to her biological parents, not Mark and Terry Wilmot). So, I was undeveloped physically and mentally (a fabrication of sorts) Not only that, I did crack my head open at the age of eleven or twelve (Kandice never cracked her head open but did experience a minor sports injury which required stitches). That made things worse for me.

In another of her letters recovered and preserved for the trial, Kandice writes;

Dear Nick,

I am sorry for this letter. This time will be the last. I know you have fallen in love with me. I don't know if it is for the best. I lost everything, and I can't risk losing you too. You're going to run after me . . .you're going to cry. You're going to be so depressed.

With everyday I'm with you, I'm losing. I miss you, and never have enough. I feel so sick of being selfish. I can't live this way. Seeing girls fall at your feet. You don't see them, but I can't deal with the jealousy anymore.

I lie every night and think what am I doing. Is this for love, vengeance, or self-moral?

I'm not sure myself anymore. We have been together for one year and four months now. It was wonderful, but I just can't take the pain anymore.

Your friend, Kandice Wilmot

P.S. Never believe what I write, not supposed to ever be sent, read, or copied!

My Intent & Effort Was Always Honorable

So, now after all I've written, and all the background information provided, everyone should be able to grasp how a teenage girl, who has been wrongly labeled, and turned into a victim, becomes what people have made her. This young girl has been allowed to believe she has been abused, in fact, she has been encouraged to believe it. Now she plays out the role in what becomes an even sadder state of affairs.

I could continue writing about this affair, dissecting more of the details, however, it's all become mentally and physically exhausting. I carry the weight of the injustice and idiotic madness with me everywhere, every day, and every night. Worse yet, the toughest part of the fight still lies ahead – a courtroom battle featuring the Commonwealth of Massachusetts versus Mark Wilmot, the freedom fighter. For that reason, it's time to try to bring this book to an end, but will this nightmare ever end?

I've demonstrated through my investigation and observations that the allegations against me were fabrications, and that the social service system, and most of the public servants involved, destroyed a family while taking life, liberty, and the pursuit of happiness away from a good man. No one ever taught me everything there is to know about how to become a good man, or a good father. I figured much of it out on my own, and did my best with the tools on hand. When it comes to my family and country, I can say this with confidence;

✶My intent has always been honorable, and my effort has been commendable. Besides teaching my children well, I made contributions to society, and planned to do even more for the greater community. My life's work has been disrupted. It's not right, or just as to what has been done to my family, and it's not fair that my status of a father has been tainted, and that my honor has been stolen – remember, I served the United States of America as a world-wide freedom fighter, trained to seek out and destroy the enemy of freedom with extreme prejudice, so that others could enjoy the benefit of liberty.

✶All the social service agency workers, with their educations, theories, and conventional wisdom, can never match my wife and my efforts at raising kids, or our cumulative experience unless they can show they took care of ten or more children. They should never have inserted themselves into our family. They suffer from institutional group-think, and the detriments of idiocy.

THE IDIOCY CONTINUES AS A FATHER IS PROSECUTED

Despite all the evidence that indicated that abuse did not occur in the Wilmot home, the truth behind the fiasco never came out over the fourteen months following the Mother's Day attack on the Wilmot parents. Instead, the Commonwealth of Massachusetts continued its intervention into the lives of family members, spending over one-hundred thousand dollars of the taxpayer's money in the process. That money was not spent in a positive way as one would hope, but instead, was used to break apart a functioning family unit, to destroy the father's life and reputation, to prosecute an innocent man, and to destabilize the two young girls who were already children at risk because of problems which occurred before they were adopted by Mark and Terry Wilmot. In other words, the idiocy behind the attack on a loving family, with two members who served their country as Marines continued. A trial date was set for July 19, 2010, at the East Brookfield Courthouse. On that date, Mark Anthony Wilmot, a man who had never been arrested or detained by police, a decorated hero, a father of four, a man who was honorably retired as a Marine Corps Master Sergeant, a man who was certified as a foster parent, and screened as an adoptive parent, would be prosecuted by the Commonwealth of Massachusetts on trumped up charges of abuse.

The initial allegation made on Mother's Day 2009 purported that Mark A. Wilmot had sexually, physically, and mentally assaulted his two girls over a period of ten years. Evidence to substantiate that behavior was never presented or found because it did not exist. It did not exist because Mark Wilmot did not abuse his children. All state officials could do, with their vast resources and teams of so-called professionals who claim to want to help families and ensure justice, was to conduct a fishing expedition. Once the fishing expedition was over, they displayed their catch, claiming there was sufficient reason to charge the father with one count of assault and battery against each girl, and one count of indecent assault, where it was claimed that a father of four had once touched the buttock of one of his daughters when she was eight-years old. Yes, the idiocy that the author of this record of events claimed to exist when he began writing this book, does exist, and not just in this case, but throughout the entire system, which was put into place to prevent child abuse, and help families.

The Cost Of A Defense Is Too High

When word got out that I was going to defend myself in a criminal trial, people close to me began to feel uncomfortable, saying it was a risky and dangerous to defend oneself in a criminal trial. Feeling as strong as I do about my innocence, and freedom and justice, and the country itself, I felt I had no choice but to defend myself. Don't get me wrong – if I had twenty-thousand dollars cash, and I could somehow locate a team of competent lawyers, then I would let them perform the task, however, that option was not available as the family's finances completely fell apart.

Instead of having a team of lawyers perform the work, I prepared myself for the worst case scenario, meaning I was ready to go to jail if I had too. I did not fear that outcome, I merely anticipated that if that were to happen, I would make the best of it by making new friends, helping people to read and write better, and, at the same time, providing spiritual leadership to men in jail. While getting ready for trial, I kept a certain level of confidence in regular, average people, believing that if I could speak face to face with a jury, and provide the evidence which had existed all along, that the truth would come out, and I would be found not guilty.

As the trial date came closer, I studied the legal process by researching the law and trial procedures on the internet.

I also adjusted my attitude, meaning, that as angry as I was, I understood that I could not come across as an individual who was furious that his life and family had been unjustly taken away. I had to be nice and calm and respectful, even to the people who were trying to convict me of crimes against the children whom I had taken such good care of.

The week before the trial, I wrote and delivered a letter to the Assistant District Attorney, stating right up front that I would be respectful of him, the court, and all legal traditions.

In an effort to ensure a sense of fair play, I also volunteered to provide copies of all information gathered during the past fourteen months, including an early version of this book. There was nothing to hide. I hoped the Assistant District Attorney would reciprocate in this sincere effort to create an environment of fair play where the truth could be laid out for all to see. I still had hope that some responsible adult, such as the District Attorney, would come to their senses by asking each other what the heck were they doing. This never happened, so the people involved remained focused on pressing charges against me, an action by local and state government which still baffles many people to this day, especially considering how good a father I had been, and the effort I had put forth in parenting Kandice and Davalia.

The letter I wrote to the prosecutor, with its implied offer of complete cooperation was met with silence. This reaction revealed what he was thinking – no doubt he reviewed the information, including the evidence and witness list I provided, then made a decision to win the trial by taking advantage of my ignorance compared to his education, experience, and technical knowledge of the legal process. The prosecutor did not anticipate, nor could he have comprehended that Josey Wales was riding again, this time not in the movie, but in the sense that a man and a family had been done wrong. Nor did the prosecutor understand that he was entering a battle against a United States Marine who had been unjustly attacked – that a gross injustice was laid upon that Marine's feet, and that honor and integrity was at stake. So the courtroom battle would come down to respect verse arrogance. Of course it was also a fact that a large number of people were praying for me.

The prosecutor did not realize it, nor did he care that I had vowed "to set things right," and furthermore, that I viewed the trial as just one battle in many more to come. My determination to set things right had continued to grow during the fourteen months when I was deprived of my life, liberty, and pursuit of happiness.

I had no intention of resting until the public servants were held accountable for their unprofessional, negligent actions, and the injustice was corrected. Based on these conditions, the District Attorney could never win the trial.

DCF Official Says Constitution Does Not Apply

During the discovery process, I personally visited, and requested in writing, on two occasions, copies of all records from the Department of Children and Families' Blackstone Valley office. I was subsequently contacted by their attorney, who told me that they would not comply with legal requirements of discovery, and most alarming, that his agency was not bound by Constitutional Law, and that my rights did not take precedence. This statement in itself, speaks volumes about arrogance of an agency which is out of control, and the delicate condition of liberty in the United States.

A FATHER DEFENDS HIMSELF

With many questions surrounding this affair left unanswered, I did indeed have to go into criminal court on July 19, and July 20, 2010 at which time I refuted the charges of abuse during a two-day trial. Sure enough, the prosecutor attempted to convict me of criminal acts against my children, not with real evidence, but with his expertise of the legal system and the false information that had been assembled through a combination of bias, prejudice, negligence, and professional malpractice. And do you know what? Not one person from the Department of Children and Families was present during this trial, meaning that I had attended court on more than ten occasions while the people who caused the costly injustice, police officers and social service workers, did not attend one single hearing. What is wrong with this scenario?

Most Evidence Is Blocked By The State

During the early stages of the trial, the prosecutor raised objections to approximately twenty-seven of the thirty-six items of evidence that I had prepared to defend myself. Unfortunately, the judge agreed with him. Believe it or not, I was denied the opportunity to introduce as evidence, the fabricated allegation of abuse written by Michelle, and the erroneous police records check, both which were used to start, and then build the criminal case against me.

The prosecutor also prevented the introduction of the official 51A, 51B, and Family Net reports from the Department of Children and Families. These three official documents, with input from various sources, including social workers, were important because they contained interview results and comments from teachers, counselors, and the girl's pediatricians stating there was no sign of abuse or neglect of Kandice and Davalia Wilmot.

By preventing the introduction of factual items of evidence which I had carefully gathered for the trial, the prosecutor neutralized my strategy to show the jury how false allegations and a foxy scheme, followed up by bias, prejudice, and negligence, had led to the trumped up charges being filed against me. So, instead of relying on factual, documented evidence which would reveal the truth, I was forced to rely on the testimony of witnesses, and the intellect of the jury to arrive at a verdict.

The State Threatens A Friendly Witness

The jury consisted of six men, and one woman. Before the start of the trial, I was able to participate in their selection. I ignored convention wisdom, and instead selected a good cross selection of people, several of whom had some type of experience in social services, and medical and technical fields. One of the men stated he had a brother who had been convicted of indecent assault of a relative, one man was a social worker, and one man was in law enforcement.

The course of the trial took sudden turns, but I did not lose my composure. As a Marine, I was prepared for sudden changes in the midst of battle field. This was a classic example of the fog of war – things would constantly change, so I had to be ready to adapt and overcome.

If you recall, Davalia, the youngest daughter had recanted her claim of abuse one-year earlier, however, people at the District Attorney's office, including the new prosecutor, who had been exposed to the poison of the well-written fabrication by Michelle, and the erroneous police records check, chose to ignore the information brought to the surface by Davalia, even though it supported my claims of innocence which I had made from day one. The public officials, even the pretty court advocate who displayed a constant attitude that she had it all figured out and knew I was guilty, were all convinced I was a bad guy.

By this stage, even if Kandice and Davalia both recanted the tale of abuse, the proverbial well had been poisoned to such a great degree that everyone who drank from it without caution would continue to believe that Mark Wilmot of North Oxford was a bad father who abused his children over and over again in every manner possible.

When the prosecutor (re)discovered that Davalia would actually testify on my behalf, and admit to the court that a scheme by three angry young girls started the allegations, and that she would deny that abuse took place, she was taken aside by the victim advocate who gently suggested she could be charged with perjury. In doing so, the state intimidated a witness, preventing her from testifying, which is a chargeable offense. The DA's office did not view this as acting illegally, rather they viewed themselves as people above the law, and viewed their action as a strategic move to win the case. Believing that he could convict me without the testimony of Davalia, the prosecutor administratively dropped one of the charges of assault and battery against that child, dropped her from involvement in the trial, then pressed full-speed ahead on the other two counts of assault and battery against Kandice.

Davalia and her boyfriend Gage, whom officers had brought to the Oxford police station, and directed under duress to produce an inflammatory statement against Mark Wilmot, were scheduled as witnesses in the trial, however, when it became evident that their testimony would support Mark Wilmot's claim of innocence, the prosecutor stopped the pair from participating as prosecution witnesses to focus on getting a conviction on the remaining charges of assault against Kandice.

Davalia recanted her story of abuse a full one-year before the trial. She also disclosed that Michelle coached both girls into building up the allegations, then instructed them to study notes on the way to the police station so their stories would match. After learning that Davalia's testimony would benefit her father's defense, the prosecutor dropped the single charge of assault and battery involving Davalia, and declined to have her testify during the trial.

Michelle Does Not Show Up In Court To Testify

On July 18th, the day before the trial, Kandice, the older of the two girls, stated she no longer wished to testify against her father. The following day, she made a choice not to attend the trial, and stayed home in bed as her mother and sister left the house. As the trial got underway, the prosecutor objected to this unexpected absence of a witness, so he asked the judge to have someone drive out to North Oxford to get Kandice, pick her up, then force her to appear in court. The trial was temporarily adjourned so this could happen.

In the absence of a subpoena, or a warrant to appear in court, the state was directing without cause that a juvenile family member be compelled to testify against her will, a violation of the law, as well as a violation of a person's rights. That did not matter. Again, the people involved view themselves as above the law.

When the trial resumed two hours later, Kandice became the state's first, and only witness. The District Attorney's office chose not to bring Michelle into court as a witness, or anyone else, not even the officer who filed the criminal complaint, or the three primary social service workers, or a DCF supervisor. Now, why would that be?

The Jury Is Warned About Perception vs Reality

During my opening statement, given while standing face to face with the jury, I invested a few minutes of time describing how the case they were about to hear was less about child abuse, and more about idiocy, gross negligence, and the void which can exist between perception and reality. In essence, jury members received a mental inoculation. This cautionary inoculation built up their intellectual strength against the maladies of corrupt thought which could possibly affect anyone when they reach conclusions based on perceptions which are not anchored in reality. This pre-emptive warning was critically important because I had already been prevented from introducing the majority of the items of evidence which would reveal the whole truth of the matter before the entire court. Now that the jury was mentally inoculated, and equally skeptical of both sides, they would be able to recognize when they were being misled by people's perceptions.

Kandice Takes The Witness Stand

Sadly, I had been forbidden to see Kandice since Mother's Day 2009. That was over one year ago. I was prevented from protecting her during the same period. The truth is that the Commonwealth of Massachusetts had replaced me as a parent, taking over the reigns of the Wilmot household as they turned an honorable man and good father into a homeless disabled veteran whose name was now listed on the state's secret alleged perpetrator list.

As Kandice entered the courtroom, and strode toward the witness stand, no one on the jury knew that she was a bright child who fondly pursued the fantasy world of the Wiccan religion, or that she had run away from home during the past year, or that she had spent time in a youth lock-down facility, or that a psychiatrist had prescribed her medication, or that she was now pregnant at the age of sixteen years, all developments which took place in the absence of her father.

The jury did not even know the details of her early life because that was all considered irrelevant. The only thing the jury knew was that the prosecutor had presented a case claiming Kandice Wilmot had been abused by her father, and that abuse was presented in the form of two incidents.

Everyone in the courtroom was intrigued as Kandice confidently walked to the left-center of the legal box to take the witness stand. I anticipated her performance would be truly theatrical on account of her comfort level, and proven ability to make good first impressions.

True to my prediction, Kandice showed she had poise, and demonstrated that she was not shy, (Michelle had claimed both girls were shy, and therefore were being abused) nor did she have any fear when it came to a new circumstance such as standing on the witness stand in front of a group of strangers. In this unusual environment, most children would feel awkward, and a bit shy, or a bit reserved, and maybe even a little nervous, but not Kandice.

The prosecutor proceeded to ask her questions in the rapid, practiced fashion of a seasoned professional. During his opening statement, before I had given mine, the prosecutor had resurrected the story line which was woven together and maliciously crafted by Michelle and the two young girls during May of 2009.

As the prosecutor repeated the accusations, he was portraying me as someone I wasn't – an abusive parent. As he did this, I reminded myself of the advice my five sisters had given me last December, just as I was departing the annual family Christmas party. Each of them hugged me, just as they always have, then one of them said; *"Mark, just continue to be who you are."* Those words of support were powerfully meaningful, and went a long way from December to this day in court as I sat quietly while the public servants continued wasting taxpayer money in a grand act of idiocy and injustice.

When you first hear a case laid out by an official in court, it always sounds believable, after all, it's natural to assume that some combination of events must have caused the gathering of people in the court room. The prime defect to the prosecutor's presentation to the jury was that he had zero evidence to back up his case. There were zero historical reports of even one incident of abuse, zero reports of injuries, zero medical reports, no police incident reports, and no witnesses to verify any incident of abuse. The Commonwealth's case was based on perceptions – which had been initially triggered by teenager rebellion and anger, and the resentment and embellishments of an impaired young woman, then further fueled by people's bias and lack of professionalism which existed in a wide realm of idiocy.

A Wrongful Prosecution

The image of a dis-honorable and abusive parent was presented to the jury, clashing in sharp contrast to the reality of the man defending himself on defense stand, and the reality of the excellent home life that Terry and Mark Wilmot had provided to their adopted children.

The bottom line was that the Commonwealth lacked sufficient evidence to justify the prosecution of Master Sergeant Mark A.

Wilmot, i.e., it was a wrongful prosecution – a case that should never have gone to court.

The District Attorney, along with Kandice's agreements to his line of questioning, portrayed me as a dishonorable man who slapped his kids around, grabbed their ass, and abused them by dragging them around by their hair and slamming their heads against the walls. As a matter of formality during this process, at the request of the District Attorney, Kandice identified me as the person who had abused her in this manner.

Kandice Reveals Her Strengths To The Jury

Once the prosecutor completed his presentation, and his direct line of questioning, it became time for the defense to cross-examine the Commonwealth's star witness. I came to my feet, and walked over to stand beside the jury because I saw that is what the prosecutor did. I remained there while cross-examining Kandice.

I began the cross-examination by asking Kandice if it was true that she had the ability to read notes and memorize things with good effectiveness. She replied yes. I asked her if she could play music instruments, and sing, and act on stage. She replied yes. I asked her if she studied notes on the way to the police station on Mother's Day. She said yes.

Next came a seemingly harmless question; "Kandice, are you a good actress?"

Kandice paused ever so slightly, smiled, then laughed, and replied, "No!" in her angelic acting voice. This was a classic moment because Kandice provided the perfect answer to the question about her acting ability; in answering the way she did, she demonstrated to the jury how good of an actress she really was. She *acted* naturally, and brilliantly, as if she was a modest, humble person, when in fact, her reactive exuberance, and her humble negative response revealed her true talent as an actress.

**Kandice sits on the couch with her boyfriend
one month before Mother's Day 2009**

This awakened the jury's curiosity as they instantly became acutely aware of the complexities of the case, and the possibility that the witness before them was not a consistently reliable source of accurate information.

I continued asking Kandice questions, inquiring if she had a disagreement with me on one occasion when I picked her up at school, when we discussed Albert Einstein while traveling home. She said yes. I continued, inviting her to share more about the basis of the argument;

"Did you disagree with me over why, and how Albert Einstein came to the United States before World War I, and did you get out of the truck when we arrived home, then shout at me;

["I'm sick and tired of you always thinking your are right, and I'm not going to take it anymore!"]? (While slamming the door shut)

At this point, Kandice replied yes again, but then she elaborated further without an invitation to do so, in a manner which again revealed her true colors. With enthusiastic sunshine, Kandice expanded on her answer;

"Actually the argument was really about who invented the atomic bomb. You said Albert Einstein didn't invent it, and I said he did, and I proved that you were wrong, and I was right."

Her casual, and completely comfortable, but combative testimony demonstrated that she was not an abused child living in any type of fear, but that she was a bright, determined girl who was intent on being right, and a well-spoken young lady who would stop at nothing to get her point across, and in this case, winning this battle against her father who always tried to keep her safe and under control.

Final Witness Comments Reveal Motives

As the afternoon of the first day grew late, I called my wife Terry, and my two great sons as witnesses. I can't stress enough on the pages of this book how proud I was to have them there because their presence alone spoke volumes about whom I was as a husband and a father. The essence of their testimony was that I was a father who hugged his children every day, and a father who looked out for them in every possible way. All three testified that Kandice and Davalia were never abused, and they never saw any abuse, and if there was any abuse going on, they would have stepped in to stop it. It's a real shame no one from social services or the Oxford Police Department was present to hear this testimony. It would have been good for them to see it, and to hear it.

The Godmother of Kandice and Davalia, Debbie Kempton, the older sister of Terry was also called in to testify. A curious fact about Debbie, is she is married to Stephen Kempton. Steve had been an active, high level member of the Exchange Club, almost going all the way to National President of the community service organization. The ironic aspect about this fact is that Steve was an expert on child abuse. He had spoken repeatedly on the subject, and ran programs on the topic. If anyone suspected that Kandice and Davalia had been abused by their father, it would be Debbie and Steve, both of whom had frequent contact with both girls.

Debbie was always around Kandice and Davalia, and if anything had ever happened to them, she too would have known it because she was so close to them. She was the last witness, and it was the last question to her which provided the nail in the coffin of the Commonwealth's case. I simply asked Debbie to recount to the court what had transpired on July 10, 2009 while she was transporting Kandice back home to Thayer Pond.

Now before I relay what Kandice said, I have to first mention that Debbie had also witnessed Kandice's reaction one week earlier to the news that the police were going to try to arrest her father over the Fourth of July weekend. Without any remorse, or sadness, or concern, Kandice laughed out loud, thinking it was funny that her father was going to go to jail. A week later, while Debbie was driving toward Thayer Pond with Kandice in the front passenger seat, Kandice observed her father's white pick-up truck, and became instantly enraged;

Debbie, with sadness in her heart, proceeds to tell the jury what transpired in her car on July 9th by saying;

"Kandice saw her father's truck. She became very angry, slamming her fist onto the dashboard of my car. As she did it, she said; ["I stabbed my father in the heart, and I'll stab my mother in the back."]"

Debbie tearfully finished up by explaining that she was concerned for the safety of her sister Terry after that incident, and that she warned Terry to "watch her back."

THE VERDICT

This question lingers; how does a man have liberty, justice, and freedom after his family and life have been taken away?

After witness testimony concluded, the trial ended for the day. We reconvened the next morning, at which time I was allowed to give a closing argument to the jury. Again, I knew I better do an excellent job because it was quite possible that any single segment of the trial could turn out to be the deciding factor. During the first day, the prosecutor demonstrated he was not playing games – he would not, and did not show any restraint. He was an expert, and I was an amateur, so I took all of it seriously, executing my legal duties as best as I could.

After about four minutes of my closing statement, the judge became unhappy with what I was saying to the jury. He unexpectedly stopped the trial, then ordered the bailiff to escort the jury out of the courtroom. Once the jury members left, the judge proceeded to admonish me for not sticking to the evidence which was presented during the trial. I stood at attention and listened to his lecture, respectfully responding to his warnings.

Once he was done with the admonishment, the jury was brought back in and seated. I skipped over my planned remarks, and hastily completed the closing argument by again mentioning my earlier reference to perception verse reality. Finally, I asked then jury to find me not guilty. It was difficult to figure out what members of the jury were thinking. They all sat very still. Each person maintained an expressionless face. No one could figure out what they were thinking, or how they would vote.

By legal tradition, the prosecutor had the right of the last argument. He stood up, and went right at it, again drawing on his confidence and his experience to achieve victory. He did not hold anything back, in fact, he was ruthless. He rapidly spoke about how Kandice had always told the truth, even when it did not fit her well, then he rehashed how I had committed crimes against her, especially the charge of touching her buttock when she was eight years old, and how she remembered it because she referenced the movie she was watching at the time.

When the prosecution rested its case, the judge spent about thirty minutes, carefully going over instructions for the jury. Those instructions included the standards that must be met by the Commonwealth in trying their case. I appreciated this effort very much as the judge repeatedly told the jury to remember that a defendant remained innocent until the state proved him guilty, and furthermore, that guilt had to be proven beyond a reasonable doubt.

They took less than one hour to reach verdicts on the two remaining assault charges. One of those charges was considered a felony, so the possibility existed that I would be immediately sent off to jail if found guilty. I remained calm as everyone was seated in the courtroom. The courtroom grew quiet. The judge asked the jury foreman if they had reached a verdict on the two counts, at which time the foreman twice responded; "THE JURY FINDS THE DEFENDANT NOT GUILTY."

It was a tremendously sweet victory, however the quest of justice for a man done wrong, would have to, out of necessity, continue well into the future.

Nurtured & Protected

**Times of joy and togetherness – a boat ride on
Thayer Pond before their family was broken apart**

The two young girls involved in this story were well-cared for
until local and state authorities got involved. They were loved,
nurtured, protected, and guided up to the day the government
intruded upon their lives. If they have been abused, it's not by their
parents, but by public servants working within a bad system
without checks and balances, and without a foundation in law.

After the state intervened, both girls ran away from home, and
then, they were sent to lock-down facilities, where they were given
prescription medicines. This is the truth. Davalia ended up going
to juvenile court, and was assigned a probation officer. Kandice
became pregnant with two children at the age of sixteen. Both
these girls suffer now because of public servants who were out of
control, and operating where they were not needed, and operating
where they did not belong. Both girls will continue paying a price
well into their future because the idiocy of liberalism in
government policy destroyed their family. At the same time, their

father, who was the head of the household, their provider, and the strongest positive influence in their life, is forced out of their life. So it's the children who will be negatively affected, as will the reputation of the good man known as their father. His honor has been stolen.

This Family Will Pay A Price Well Into The Future

The government agents or public servants, whatever you want to call them, violated our family rights, and our constitutional rights. Their actions are contrary to the principles of justice and law. It adds up to a monumental gross injustice. With that said, I must seek justice, retribution, and restitution, then work toward making sure this tragedy does not happen again to someone else.

The Wilmot family, and Mark Wilmot in particular will have to endure substantial costs well into the future. Expenses for the family began adding up with temporary lodging and meals, and additional milage traveled by Mark Wilmot when he was forced out of his home by threats made by Agent Polenski, and court directives stemming from the false allegation. There are other expenses; While the girls were under the jurisdiction of the Department of Children and Families, their cell phone use skyrocketed, coming in at over seven-hundred dollars during June. Then came the costs of counseling, and traveling to and from the appointments, so of course Terry was not able to return to work full-time as planned after recovering from elbow surgery.

Another expense is the cost of legal representation, and the time off from work to attend to those details. During this period, while the unexpected burden is being placed on the family, the family has endured a loss of income by Mark Wilmot because his office was located in the garage of the Wilmot home.

Without access to his office and equipment, he has not been able to earn money while continuing the development of the books and sport concept he had been working on. Meanwhile, Terry could not return to work full-time as planned because she has to be on hand to attend court hearings, counseling sessions, and take care of the home visits conducted by social service workers.

On the evening of February 22nd, 2010, the family's mini-van was repossessed in the middle of the night, indicating the family had become totally unviable in an economic sense, thanks to the government being involved where it does not belong. The downward spiral of this family would continue for at least another year - while the people who caused it to happen received paychecks from the public coffers, and had the right to return home to their families each night.

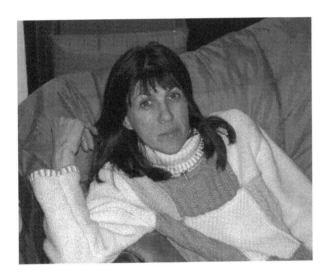

As a mother, and as an American citizen, Theresa Wilmot deserved better treatment from social workers and polices – she deserved to have her parental rights and authority respected, and her family left intact, but that's not what she got, instead she received fourteen months of intervention into her home while her husband was driven away by unaccountable social workers.

A REAL MAN CAN'T BE REPLACED

The truth of the matter is that Kandice both enjoyed and benefitted from a supportive, appropriate relationship with her father, who was a sincere man who guided her as a good parent does until the day when that relationship was undermined and ended by negligence and professional malpractice of public servants.

OBSERVATIONS ON ATTORNEYS AND THE COURTHOUSE CULTURE

My wife and I hired a reputable attorney by viewing the yellow pages, and selecting a firm with a full-page ad. Not knowing any better, and hoping for the best, we waited for action and results. We waited patiently, partly in fear, partly in ignorance, waiting for the attorney to perform his duties. This was our mistake. We should have been in constant contact with him, at least three times a week. That may have been impossible because he was a busy man, always in court with some other client. It turned out that this attorney, and others like him are participants in a system and culture that is not functioning as well as it should be, except perhaps for the people employed by it. As the trial date approached, I felt very much under-served and alienated by our attorney, so on June 22, 2010, less than one month before the trial, I wrote to the judge, requesting permission to drop the attorney so I could defend myself. Permission was granted.

Assessing The Performance of Public Servants

In the weeks leading up to the trial, I had to make several trips to the court clerk's office to file documents, or to ask for information. The clerks at the Dudley District Court, and the man in charge of the office were attentive to their duties, and respectful and helpful to citizens as they stood as customers at the office counter. This was in stark contrast to the East Brookfield courthouse, where an environment of fear existed. One of the clerks there was very kind and helpful, however she appeared almost afraid to help the public too much because of the culture which had developed there. At least one of the supervisors in charge of the clerk's office presented a barrier to good service.

This person was incredibly uncooperative, and consistently feigned ignorance of basic legal issues, and may have been intentionally stonewalling during my quest for justice, which, if true, would be corruption. For example, when I asked how to go about asking for permission to defend myself in the upcoming criminal trial, the office manager casually and defensively instructed me to just show up. Of course this was not true, as defendants in criminal trials are required to request and obtain permission from the judge before defending themselves.

The supervisor's un-willingness to be helpful, and her less than enthusiastic attitude towards serving the public is another instance of public servants forgetting whom they work for. This particular person, no doubt well-paid in a senior position, works for the taxpayer, that's you and me. In this instance, it was a father in legal jeopardy, who was standing at the counter seeking much-needed help. The manager had not been reminded of this fact. A culture of excellence had not developed, so service with a smile was not part of the daily plan as I visited the East Brookfield court clerk's counter numerous times during July of 2010.

In place of a keen awareness of accountability to the public, there existed an attitude of arrogance and corruption. That in turn caused me to lose confidence in the fidelity of the clerk's office. This condition is reality, not perception, so I had to hope for the best each time I went to the counter. I was so disappointed after the final conversation with the court clerk because I had requested that the FBI, the Onslow County Sheriff, and the Onslow County Department of Social Services provide information to the court before the trial. This information was faxed to the clerk's office, and should have been included in the case file. When I asked the senior clerk to confirm the information had arrived, she curtly stated she would have shredded it because she did not keep "that kind of information around," especially if no one told her it was coming. This is all true. Hopefully by sharing it with readers, and elected officials change will begin taking place, not just in social services, but in the court system too.

IMPORTANT NOTE: During the discovery process, I also personally visited, and requested in writing, on two occasions, copies of all records from the Department of Children and Families' Blackstone Valley office. I was subsequently contacted by their attorney, by telephone, who informed me that they would not comply with legal requirements of discovery, and most alarming, that his agency was not bound by Constitutional Law, and that my rights did not take precedence over state law. This statement in itself, speaks volumes about arrogance of an agency which is out of control, and the delicate condition of liberty in the United States.

Improvement Can Be Achieved By Leadership

In reality, my wife and I were two people outside the system and the courthouse culture – just another set of clients who would come and go, passers-by, as if we were riding an escalator like the escalators installed inside large airports, except this people-mover travels through the courthouse every few months with a new batch of citizens. The unwise come and go, while in-the-know attorneys remain privileged fixtures within the connected courthouse culture, where they merrily banter back and forth with fellow professionals, including court officials, whom they become familiar with on a daily basis. Much of this can be blamed on human nature, however this condition fosters complacency of many people working within the system, and a tendency to expedite the process of justice through the making of deals with a nod and a wink, in place of drawn-out battles, or outright dismissals where unconstitutional actions, corruption, negligence, and silliness might be exposed.

The only way this system is going to change for the better is through awareness of cases such as the Wilmot's, and through accountability and improved, sustained leadership by those people placed in charge of the courthouse system.

WHO WILL BE HELD ACCOUNTABLE?

Now you've read this book, you have had time to absorb the truth and consequences of state-sponsored actions, or state-sponsored terrorism, whichever phrase you believe fits best. Throughout this story, many overhead questions were raised, so now it's time for you to be the judge, to answer those overhead questions to determine if it is legal and morally acceptable for public servants to wage hostile attacks against family units, and to determine if it is acceptable for the government to show up at the home of a United States Marine, destroy a good man and his family which took twenty-eights years to build, and then just walk away.

To me, the answers are quite obvious – it's all unacceptable, and it can't be allowed to stand.

It's A Mission Which Must Be Accomplished

I'm taking the fight right back to the very people involved in this action, and the people who allow it to happen to others. When this case goes to Federal Court during 2011, people involved must be held personally accountable. Ultimately, someone will answer, then pay for the collateral damage done to the two adopted girls, their father, their mother, their brothers, their grandparents, their aunts and uncles, and their God parents, which all made up the gem of a family they once had.

I expect individuals who contributed to this injustice to be terminated for cause. I plan to identify those people by name to the courts, to the public, and to the vast network of military veterans around the country. I will demand letters of apology for my wife, my sons, and myself. Furthermore, I will seek considerable restitution and compensation for my family and myself.

★★★As I pledged in the very beginning, I will cause change to a social "service" system that is dysfunctional, unresponsive, and unaccountable to the public. The madness of destroying families in order to help them must end. The sloppy investigations, the witch hunts, the adversarial approach, and the persecutions of wrongly accused men must stop. The natural rights of all parents, and the sovereignty of the family unit in a free society must be recognized, upheld, and protected. Most importantly, constitutional rights, with an emphasis of equal protection under the law, must be adhered to.

★With the above objectives in mind, I have already visited the United States Attorney's office, as well as the Federal Bureau of Investigation's office in Boston, Massachusetts in order to request assistance from the federal government. I have also contacted the American Civil Liberties Union for additional support, and they put me in contact with an important person who may be viewed as a subject matter expert on civil actions against the Department of Children and Families.

This is not a fight that I choose to take on, but rather a fight I must take on. In one of several civil law suits to be filed in federal district court, my legal team will lay out a coherent legal presentation in front of a judge and jury of Americans, to explain why following the Constitution means maintaining *fidelity* to the law, while respecting and protecting the rights of every individual.

Once the framework of the freedom that our Nation was founded upon is renewed in the minds of those present, my legal team will move forward to prove that government agents abused the powers of their office, acted negligently, and perhaps criminally, broke laws, and repeatedly violated my rights, especially my Fifth Amendment Rights, by depriving me of life, liberty, property, and the pursuit of happiness without due process of the law, and the Sixth Amendment, by not informing me of the nature and cause of the accusations against me, and by not providing me with a speedy trial in which I could defend myself before the Wilmot family was destroyed and my life was ruined. From what I have been able to determine, there are more than twenty flagrant violations of civil rights in this matter.

This federal court case will highlight, and demonstrate that state laws concerning the handling of alleged abuse of children must be reviewed for constitutionality, and that procedures must be changed to include a genuine concern for parent's rights, a man's reputation, the future of the family unit, and family members involved.

Finally, people hired to perform duties in this line of social work must be thoroughly schooled in the fact that they are not above the law, that they are public servants paid with tax dollars from their clients, and finally, that their job is to preserve family units rather than destroy them.

Although a monetary figure could never be placed on the damages done to the lives and reputations of the Wilmot family, the monetary award stemming from this pending federal civil lawsuit will be substantial enough to meet Kandice and Davalia's future needs, and great enough to somehow compensate Terry, Donald, Preston, and myself for our tremendous loss. The law allows for certain types of damages in a civil action, including;

❑   General damages for what the law presumes follows the type of injury that is the basis of the lawsuit

❑   Punitive damages awarded in addition to actual damages to punish defendants for their wanton, reckless, malicious, or deceitful conduct

❑   Discretionary damages for mental anguish and pain and suffering, which are not definitive

❑ Expectation damages for what an injured party reasonably anticipated receiving from an uncompleted transaction

❑ Compensatory damages for actual, proven out-of-pocket costs associated with the injury

When justice is achieved in this case, and when I have helped to set things right, the awards assigned by civil court actions must be significant enough to generate publicity, and a high-profile news story that will cause all cities, towns, counties, and states to make it a priority to immediately review and change policies which are based on past idiocy and malpractice. Furthermore, this court victory will cause all employees serving in roles as public servants, who are conducting the business of the citizens, to think twice, and to think with wisdom, before embarking on any course of action, which is contrary to common sense, fairness, and principles of freedom that America was founded upon.

Please Help: Write Letters & Talk To People
Please consider ways that you can help defend liberty in the United States, especially by working to prevent the growth of government and regulation, and by working to restrict the power of public servants wherever possible.

Please provide copies of this book to others, and ask them to sign the petition asking for the repeal of all mandatory reporting laws which can be shown to have a detrimental impact of society. Remember what I repeated several times; this could happen to you or a member of your family. Take action. Discuss this issue with all of your local public servants and elected officials. Remind people that all families have a right to privacy and autonomy, and that men in their community need to be protected as much, if not more than any other person.

Use the power of the pen. Write to the Governor of Massachusetts, and the Commissioner of the Department of Children and Families. Tell them it's time to cut the size of the Department of Children and Families in half, and ask that drastic change begin immediately, starting with developing respect for freedom, the family unit, and the rights of every parent.

Semper Fi,

Mark A. Wilmot

Master Sergeant, United States Marine Corps (ret)
Formerly of North Oxford, Massachusetts

Governor Deval Patrick
Massachusetts State House
Office of the Governor
Room 280
Boston, MA 02133

Angelo McClain, Commissioner
Massachusetts Department of Children and Families
24 Farnsworth Street
Boston, MA 02210

Area Director/All Social Workers
Massachusetts Department of Children and Families
South Central/Blackstone Valley Office
185 Church Street
Whitinsville, MA 01588

State Senator Richard Moore
State House, Room 111
Boston, MA 02133

Senator John F. Kerry
421 Russell Senate Office Building
Washington, DC 20510

Oxford Board of Selectmen
Town Hall
Main Street
Oxford, MA 01540

KEY WORDS & PHRASES

Abuse of power

Authority

Agenda

Bias

Child abuse, definition of

Color of Law

Compelling Interest

Constitutional Rights

Context

Cognitive template

Core values

Desire to serve

Emergency condition

Family unit

Family rights

Filter

Frame of reference

Freedom

Foxy scheme

Gag Order

Group-think

Head of the household

Innocent,

    – until proven guilty

Idiocy

Judge

Judicial review

Justified use of power

Leadership

Liberty

Men's rights

Motives

Overzealous

Objective

Perspective

Perception

Prejudice

Personal judgement

Professional

Professional scrutiny

Public hysteria

Reactionary

Reality

Reckless

Respect

Reverence for family

Right To Associate

State-sponsored terror

Strict scrutiny

System-wide

Supervisor

Tendency

To Serve and Protect

Train of thought

Values

Wanton

Proof

Made in the USA
Charleston, SC
20 January 2011